ROAD TO AUGUSTA

R. B. C. Howell and the Formation of the Southern Baptist Convention

Joe W. Burton

BROADMAN PRESS

Nashville, Tennessee

This Is His Story

To the man of faith, history is His story. Properly told, the annals of time carry always the golden thread of man's quest after God and God's unceasing search for man. Find the key to unlock the meaning of any era of man's days on earth and it must ever be the record of religion, of the continuing pursuit to discover the deepest meanings.

History is His story—and it is also his story. That is, the accurate historical account is biographical. There is no possibility of understanding the American Revolution apart from the life story of its dominant personality, George Washington. And who would assume to interpret the fratricidal tragedy of American civil strife without a full disclosure of the lonely Lincoln?

On that principle, the record of the early development of Southern Baptists as a denomination will be understood only in relation to central personalities. This is not at all to affirm that Southern Baptist life in its beginning is comprehended in the career of one man. Far from it. Indeed, quite the contrary.

There are a number of men—and of families—any one of whom in his strategic lifetime embraced the salient beginnings and influenced the launching of the Southern Baptist denomination. Johnson, Jeter, Manly, Holman, Curtis, Fuller, Taylor, Sands, Mercer, Furman, DeVotie, Lumpkin, Whitsitt—these are all names, as well as that of Howell, to remind the reader of Southern Baptist history of significant contributions to the denomination's early life. Any one of them could be selected as a proper basis for a study of Southern Baptist beginnings.

At the outset—and still as necessary by way of introduction—two disclaimers must be made. The pages that follow are not intended as comprehensive history, although they are historical in content. They are not to be taken as a full, but only as a partial or limited account. Second, neither is this book a biography, although much in the pages is biographical. In a word, this is a report on the development of the Southern Baptist Convention around the career of R. B. C. Howell. The selection could as well have been any one of many other worthy representatives. It is appropriate, however, in view of the significant role that Howell filled in those exciting days. Howell is a key person at the time of beginnings, 1835-1865. The focus in these pages is on his career in its relation to the formation of the Southern Baptist Convention.

To follow will be a similar focus on two other persons in relation to succeeding eras of Convention development: Isaac Taylor Tichenor, 1850-1900; and James Marion Frost, 1880-1915. The one came at the time of reconstruction of a denomination following war's destruction, and the other in the projection of strategy for popular indoctrination. Tichenor is the man into whose sturdy hands was committed the task of calling a discouraged people together after the awful disruption of Civil War, and Frost undertook the challenge to indoctrinate a growing mass of people.

These studies, aimed at covering the development of denominational structure around the careers of these men, will be offered in three volumes. The work is sponsored by the Convention's Historical Commission, Home Mission Board, and Sunday School Board. It is my rare good fortune to be associated with these Convention agencies in this significant work.

Contents

R. B. C. Howell in the Middle Years

1

Man on a Mission

When R. B. C. Howell first laid eyes on the Great Valley in the summer of 1834, he was already convinced that the Southwest was the strategic arena for kingdom conquest. The young pastor of Cumberland Street in Norfolk had made his long journey to Nashville in reply to the appeal of a little band of dispirited Baptists in search of a pastor. Before departing from Nashville six weeks later, he knew that the Tennessee city on the Cumberland was the gateway to this imperative advance. And even as he boarded coach or boat on the return to Norfolk, he hugged to himself the blueprint of the religious newspaper that would be his chief means for taking the entire region for Christ.

Never a man indecisive as to personal involvement, Howell on his long homeward journey was atingle with one overriding thought: he himself, Robert Boyte Crawford Howell, had indeed come to the kingdom for such a time as this. His destiny was in the Southwest. His place was in the Great Valley. This conviction was impressed with every jog of the journey, at every bend of the dashing stream.

With steadfast purpose he stayed with that personal commitment to the end of his days. He gave his full life thereafter to the development of the Baptist denomination primarily in the Southwest. At the organization of the Southern Baptist Convention in Augusta in 1845, his dominant leadership strongly influenced the gathered Southern Baptists, even though for valid reason he was not present in the meeting.

Later he was absent also from Nashville for a seven-year tenure as pastor in Richmond, 1850-57, and it was precisely in those seven years that he presided at the biennial sessions of the Southern Baptist Convention. Moreover, paradoxically, at the end of those seven years of absence, he returned to the Nashville pastorate for his single most intensive service to Baptists in the Southwest and the entire South—that at the very time when by his own determination he was no longer president of the Convention.

The crisis that brought Howell back to Nashville after seven years in Virginia was again a desperate plea of need. On this new visit as prospective pastor, in 1857, Howell was aghast at how completely Landmarkism had drained the missionary spirit of Baptists in Nashville, in Middle Tennessee, and indeed throughout the Southwest. He saw the deterioration of seven short years which posed a challenge he dared not resist.

In his book, *Old Landmarkism: What Is It?*, the movement's chief advocate, J. R. Graves, wrote: "In 1846 I took charge of 'The Tennessee Baptist,' and soon commenced agitating the question of the validity of alien immersion, and the propriety of Baptists recognizing, by any act, ecclesiastical or ministerial, Pedobaptist societies or preachers as *churches* and ministers of Christ." This narrow exclusivism was the essence of early Landmarkism. Howell saw its effect on fellowship within Baptist ranks as well as on the larger Christian community. He was disturbed also at Landmark's suppression of missionary zeal.

The pernicious ecclesiastical system known as Landmarkism, centered on the banks of the Cumberland, had spread throughout the land. It became a test of fundamental denominational polity. Howell returned to Nashville to meet that challenge at the appropriate level of responsibility. He knew that within good polity an issue of difference must be resolved at the point of its occurrence.

Strangely, implementation of that polity ultimately required of Howell his resignation as president of the Southern Baptist Convention—a resignation as president in order to achieve his one most distinctive service to the Convention. Howell did both—return to Nashville and resign as president—in cordial personal compliance with his realization that his actions were in demonstration of a principle of polity that must prevail.

This bold appraisal at the outset is simply a foretoken of that which follows—of the nature of Landmarkism, its insistent spirit as to ecclesiastical forms, of principles of polity mandatory in settlement of any controversy, and also of personal cost sure to be exacted if a challenge is to be met. The forecast here simply points the way down the road ahead.

Road to Augusta goes before and beyond a Georgia meeting in 1845. It is a way to be travelled to comprehend that beginning, before and after that date and place. It includes the era of beginning. On these pages it climaxes in the early most serious threat to that beginning, when in 1859 Landmark's champion, J. R. Graves, sought to inject Landmark's threat on the floor of the Convention. To avert such an intrusion, Howell resigned the Convention presidency to bring the issue back to the local level where, by fundamental polity, the issue must be settled. Follow that Road then on these pages for a realization of its significance to an infant denominational body. And to observe some measure of R. B. C. Howell's early contribution to the Convention's preservation made possible by his clear grasp of polity.

A Beckoning Province

Back then at that beginning, look first at this mighty province that imperiously beckoned God's missionary people. The Great Valley embraced half the juvenile nation. It covered everything west of the mountains—most of it added by the Louisiana Purchase less than one short generation before. From this vast land bargain, the states of Louisiana and Missouri had already been formed, with eleven more yet to come, in whole or in part. The movement of settlers from the Seaboard states was one unending stream, all the way from the Piedmont of Georgia and the Carolinas to the rocky hills of New England.

On his homeward trek, Nashville to Norfolk, Howell met these dusty caravans. In wagons, on horseback, by river packet, and on foot they moved westward. Earlier, one family missed their young son from the marching cavalcade. Turning back, they found the boy three days later with a band of harmless Indians.

Along the way, if he had taken a direct overland route, Howell would have passed through what had been, briefly, the Free State of Franklin, but was now incorporated into the young state of Tennessee. Tennessee's state capital was not permanently fixed in Nashville on the banks of the Cumberland until 1843.

It was the great time of shifting population, from East to West, from the settled Seaboard to the Great Plains across the intervening mountains. The Southwest was being peopled with the tide of immigrants pouring through the mountain passes of Appalachia. This human throng was pitching tents, clearing the forests, building cabins, plying the streams with commerce and moving population. The new settlements must not remain destitute of the gospel.

Preachers with Bibles in their saddlebags were moving with the restless immigrants. But more were needed. Not just more in quantity but also in quality. The educated, men of maturity, ministers of established competence must be enlisted to undertake the spiritual venture. *They* must give up the security and comfort of more pleasant fields in response to the beckoning need of the newly settled and now settling Valley. This was the challenge to religious conquest in the 1830's.

There was growing concern for the spiritual welfare of the aborigines. Mounting sentiment would lead to the resettlement of Indians in newly assigned Indian Territory in the West. The Cherokees would begin in the fall of 1838 the winter march from Georgia and Carolina, every mile of the devastating journey marked by hunger, disease, bitter cold, and wholesale death. The plight of the aborigines excited the fervent missionary zeal of nineteenth-century Baptists. The Indian debacle played on the emotions. Mistreatment of one race by another cried out for rectification, as the blood of Cain's brother cried out from the ground.

But the primary missionary interest of Baptists and of all Christians at that turning time was claimed by the spiritual need of their own kinsmen in newly settled lands. The new settlements throughout the Southwest were destitute of churches. They were destitute of preachers. They were destitute of the Bible. In Nashville, for instance, Baptists had been tardy, their late, weak start following

years after the Methodists and the Presbyterians. Just six years
before Howell's first visit, the weak little Baptist congregation had
been almost completely depleted by the aggressions of a fervent
Campbellism. An adherent of the "peculiar beliefs" of Alexander
Campbell had become pastor of the Nashville church, had ingra-
tiated himself with the people, and had led almost the entire church
into the so-called Reformation preached by Campbell and his father
Thomas.

Arkansas was a wilderness. Memphis was not to have a Baptist
church until after the Civil War, when its booming population had
reached about ten thousand. In all of Texas, then a Mexican province, by diligent search one could perhaps have found two or three
churches and as many preachers of the Baptist faith. Tryon and
Huckins were not to see the Lone Star until near the end of that
decade, and Sam Houston, who later became president of the Texas
Republic, had recently settled in Texas after being sent there by
President Jackson to negotiate treaties with the Indians. (Years
later when Houston was being led down into the stream by Rufus
C. Burleson, he remembered that his wallet was still in his pocket.
"Go ahead and baptize me," he said to the pastor, "wallet and all.")

Domestic missions to Baptists in the 1830's meant establishing
the Baptist cause in the Southwest. It meant claiming for the Redeemer the vast region of the Great Valley. Baptist newspapers of
the time sounded recurringly the appeal to men with a sense of mission to go out to this new land—papers like the *Religious Herald* of
Virginia, the *Baptist Interpreter* (later the *Biblical Recorder*) of
North Carolina, *The Christian Index* of Georgia. Their warmspirited editors—Sands, Meredith, Baker—filled their columns with
news from the valley and with appeals to capable pastors to consider the call of the West.

Howell in Virginia had read these reports in the *Herald* and also
in the *Interpreter* of his native state. He, too, had written for the
same columns his own growing conviction as to the urgency of the
Southwest mission. At Norfolk as a coming young man in the
settled Tidewater, he had spoken at associational meetings and other
denominational gatherings on the present imperious challenge be-

yond the mountains. That challenge was in the spirit of the times.

Gateway to a Province

Why was Nashville the strategic gateway in the current demanding and demanded spiritual conquest of the Southwest? Why not Louisville? Or Memphis? What about St. Louis? Why not New Orleans? Or why bypass Knoxville? What about Atlanta? Or Birmingham?

The strategic significance of Nashville to the evangelization of the Southwest a century and a half ago was grounded in geographic, ethnic, economic, and human factors. Some of the factors are more readily apparent through contrast with other potential possibilities.

Knoxville, obviously, in the foothills beyond the mountains, was too near to the point of departure and not close enough to the beckoning region. Although over the mountains from the Seaboard, it was not indeed in the geographical setting of the Southwest. The same was true of Louisville. Even though the Indian Mission Association had headquarters in the Kentucky town, that location was perhaps a mistake, for there was no real geographical proximity with any of the Indian nations.

St. Louis, to be sure, was representative of the burgeoning heart of the nation. Even then the commercial center at the confluence of the Missouri and Mississippi rivers was primarily a shipping river town on the fringe of the Southwest. One traveller reported that as he passed through the town a hundred riverboats lined the busy wharfs. St. Louis became the commercial gateway to the growing West, but it was hardly to be the center of a developing spiritual empire, even though John Mason Peck since 1817 had here wrought valiantly to a wide area.

New Orleans for a generation and more was the object of continuing zeal to establish the Baptist cause. Its ethnic background as well as off-center location deprived the Crescent City of any real possibility of becoming the heart of a developing denomination.

And Memphis, while at the center of what is now known as the entrance to the Southwest, was then both far toward the outskirts of the region and had not at that time begun to develop toward its later potential. There was then no Baptist work in this new Missis-

sippi town. Birmingham, still no more than embryonic, was
founded after the war and incorporated in 1871. Atlanta, known
in 1834 as Marthasville, was given its present name in 1845 with the
coming of its first railroad.

Nashville was indeed the gateway. Water transportation, it must
be remembered, was the principal means of moving both people
and commerce. Nashville in 1834 had no railroad. Coaches did
make regularly scheduled runs through this City on the Rocks. But
a hundred riverboats frequented its docks. On the Cumberland one
could reach the Ohio, from thence the shipping lines fanned out up
the Ohio as far as Pittsburgh, down to Cairo, New Orleans, or up
from Cairo to St. Louis and Dubuque or Alton.

Howell himself had entertained the prospect of preaching in St.
Louis or New Orleans, but when the Nashville opportunity came,
he at once was captured to invest his life for Christ on the Cumberland and its environs. Thus, at the outset of a long and eventful
denominational career, R. B. C. Howell perceived the significant
relation of Nashville to the development of the people called Baptists and to his own lifetime commitment.

Yes, Nashville was the center from which over a century ago the
Baptist cause was destined to emanate like spokes in a wheel
spreading out to the farthest circumference. This Howell knew
to be true after his summer weeks in the town in 1834. The certainty of that realization gripped him increasingly on the long way
back to Norfolk.

By Means of a Paper

Before Howell left Nashville for his Norfolk home, he had already
planned to start a religious paper upon his return as pastor. This
had been a major consideration in his agreement with the church
committee. Before leaving, he had even written a prospectus and
had it published in the Nashville papers. Upon his return no time
was wasted—the first issue of *The Baptist* came from the press before
Howell and his family had resided in Nashville a month.

It is altogether likely that Howell prepared much of the copy for
this first issue on the long water journey back from Norfolk. Final

finishing touches were almost certainly given to that first copy while the family resided the first few days in the Union Hall presided over by the hospitable J. H. Marshall, whose rooms were always open without charge to preachers.

That Howell had the insight to start a paper was singular. Nothing in his experience or personal inclination indicated a bent for journalism. His motivation was neither background nor aptitude, but purely and simply a perception of the place of a paper in the work of building the Baptist cause in the Southwest.

The Baptist first came from the press in sixteen pages, in solid type, without headings and with no advertisements. It was straight reading matter, top to bottom, from beginning to end, except for the identification at the top of the first page: "The Baptist, R. B. C. Howell editor, Nashville, Tennessee, January, 1835. Published Monthly."

Howell continued as editor for thirteen years. Except for two intermissions, *The Baptist* continued in publication under the same title until 1885 when it was combined with *The Reflector*. Thus the paper Howell began in 1835 was the forerunner of the present *Baptist and Reflector*, publication of the Tennessee Baptist Convention.

The historical significance of the location of this early Baptist paper in Nashville is of more than passing interest. A number of secular papers had already appeared on the publishing horizon in Nashville's brief history. These were all in the faint beginnings of a publication industry which ultimately would serve several religious denominations. The Methodists, with their division at midcentury, moved their great publishing operation from Philadelphia to Nashville in 1854. They brought presses, type, a bindery, skilled technicians, and housed it all, men and machines, in a grand new building on the banks of the Cumberland.

Southern Baptists, skittish about setting up an ecclesiastical heirarchy to influence thought, reluctantly created a publishing board in 1891, even though they earlier had had a Sunday School Board of short duration. The Cumberland Presbyterians, Negro Baptists, Seventh Day Adventists, Disciples of Christ, Free Will Baptists

added at intervals their publishing operations to create in Nashville
a total of graphic arts industries which today is a marvel of modern
times. A modest forerunner was the 16-page solid type *Baptist*
begun by Howell in 1835.

The first newspaper in the village on the Cumberland had been
started around the turn of the century by an enterprising man named
Bradford. The very first printing press in the state had been trans-
ported by George Roulstone on horseback over the mountains from
North Carolina and put in operation at Rogersville. Roulstone not
only issued a weekly paper, the Knoxville *Gazette,* from his hand-
operated press but even published a 320-page book from hand-set
type. The tedious process of slowly gathering type line by line and
letter by letter at Rogersville and indeed the sixteen pages of *The
Baptist* were only remotely prophetic of the complex electronic and
photographic processes in Nashville's present multimillion-dollar
publishing industry.

Techniques were different but the purposes were the same:
Howell knew at the outset that the building of a Baptist empire
called for the use of an effective popular medium. This medium he
found in the printed page.

He Knew His Own Place

One other thing Howell knew for sure in 1834. He knew his own
place in the current movement to bring the Southwest into the kingdom of his Christ. There was no doubt at all in his own mind. He
came as a man fully committed to a leadership role. Everything he
did betokened this personal knowledge and acceptance of the
leadership position.

It was a leadership not of official appointment, although he came
with a year's commission from the American Baptist Home Mission
Society and in response to the call of the Nashville church. Rather,
it was from an inner certainty, on the basis of an internal acknowledgment that he came to the task. Without official appointment or
ecclesiastical designation he assumed the leadership in the Baptist
conquest of the Great Valley. It was as if he knew within himself
the role he must fulfill, and he addressed himself to it with un-

swerving confidence from the first day of his migration to the
Southwest.

Modern psychology is saying with confident insistence that self-
identification is mandatory to any kind of satisfactory living. A person must know who he is. Self-realization is always requisite to
assured, confident, victorious living. The worst confusion of all
is confusion as to one's own identity. Even the growing child in the
family is stunted and bewildered most of all by his lack of understanding of his own place in the family.

Nothing gives the poise for meaningful living as does individual
certainty as to who one is. This Howell had in the superlative. He
knew who he was. He knew his place among Baptists of the Southwest. He knew his role. He was sure of his position. His relationship was rooted firmly in self-knowledge.

We are now ready for the briefest biography of the man, which
will occupy the next chapter. It will be done briefly, as foundation
for the larger topic before us in the ensuing pages. That larger topic
is the development of a denominational polity around the career of
a key personality. That development will unfold in succeeding pages
around the career of Robert Boyte Crawford Howell. It is not the
life of Howell that will be portrayed, but the expression of
Southern Baptist polity, 1835-1865, as illustrated in the dynamic
involvement of R. B. C. Howell.

Reasons for selecting Howell as central to Southern Baptists beginnings will be made clear in the next chapter. Now it is readily
admitted that any one of a number of other key figures, or even
families, could have been selected. There was the tall, keenly perceptive parliamentarian, teacher-preacher from South Carolina,
William Bullein Johnson, who presided competently in Augusta in
1845 in the organization of the Southern Baptist Convention and
at the next two triennial sessions, 1846 and 1849.

There was the peerless preacher, Richard Fuller, pastor in the
plantation culture of the elite in Beaufort, South Carolina. He had
established himself as an avowed and ardent southerner in his famed
slavery debate by correspondence in 1844 with the illustrious
Francis Wayland. Always ready for discussion, he spoke out seven

times in one meeting to the annoyance of one editor but probably
to the delight of his own ears. His fervency was representative of a
young Baptist body.

There was Virginia's travelled J. B. Jeter, pastor in Richmond. He
had attended the recent anniversary in Providence, Rhode Island, of
the Triennial Convention. His report confirmed Southerners in the
fixed determination to form a separate organization, since there was
no hope of any reversal of the announced northern decision never to
appoint a slaveholder as a missionary or as an agent or to any other
position of trust.

Earlier there had been Georgia's Jesse Mercer. He had married a
rich widow and converted much of her wealth to Baptist endeavors.
His benefactions had led to the establishing of the famed institution
which bears his name. At Penfield he had edited *The Christian
Index.*

Others press in upon the memory in that great cloud of witnesses—J. L. Reynolds of Virginia and South Carolina, Richard Furman
and T. Curtis of the latter state, William Sands and J. B. Taylor of
Virginia, or even the witty Joseph Walker, also of Virginia, or Russell
Holman and I. T. Hinton, now struggling to establish the Baptist
cause in New Orleans, or the Manlys, father and son, of Alabama,
or any one of a dozen stalwarts in that remarkable inland town of
Marion, Alabama (H. Talbird, J. H. DeVotie, William H. McIntosh,
E. Baptist, McCraw, King, Hornbuckle). The history of the times
is replete with possibilities for the telling of history through the lives
of the illustrious. One is intrigued at the prospect of pursuing the
reading and the telling of Southern Baptist history as centered
around the lives of any one of many.

Admittedly, ours is only one of many possible selections. With
that admission, we proceed now to the announced subject.

2

By Way of Neuse and Norfolk

A name like Robert Boyte Crawford Howell would surely ever excite the interest of the curious. The first is simply a popular boy's name which appears often in the Howell strain. The second, of French derivation, came to him as a family sobriquet from his mother's side. The third crops out often even to the present generation, it having been preserved in the line of Crawford Howell, our subject's brother—who in his generation migrated to Alabama.

More typical of the man are his own claims of family background. He wrote in what he called a Memorial that his family was descended from the Tudor house of Wales. That may have been a typical assertion of pride without adequate evidence in fact. At any rate his son Morton in his own memoirs went to great length to disprove this proud claim.

Also R. B. C. claimed to be the son of a planter in Wayne County, North Carolina. Morton, after sufficient investigation to satisfy himself, said that his father was no son of a planter but of the simple farmer class, even of those who tilled the soil, often without themselves being landowners.

Any valid basis for these claims may have been lost in oral family traditions. The written accounts of father and son suggest that the younger was aware of a sometimes proud spirit on the part of his father which was capable of embellishing the scant family record.

The man with good reason was proud of honest, industrious, religious parents who gave the best training they could, limited though it was, to their numerous children. Three of the four sons became preachers. Moreover, in his mature years, this pride in his parents was augmented by some justified pride in his own personal achievements in spite of scant formal training.

The Howell family lived on a farm on the Neuse River, two miles from West Point, then the county seat of Wayne County, North Carolina. There Robert Boyte Crawford was born, March 10, 1801. He was denied college training because of the lack of money. In the "old field schools" he studied reading, writing, and ciphering until he was twenty-three. He seldom attended church because there were no churches in his community. He said that other members of his family and neighbors were not very religious.

Nearly all of his religious training came from his mother, Jane Crawford Howell. An occasional itinerant preacher visited in the community and conducted a service of exhortation. The Howells were nominal Episcopalians, as was "every other respected person" in the community. From the Bible and the Book of Common Prayer young Howell formed his own religious creed.

These studies brought him inerrantly to the conclusion that religion was wholly spiritual, received by faith through the work of the Holy Spirit in the heart, that immersion was the only true mode of baptism, and that any hierarchical form of church government was unsupported by the Word of God. These conclusions led to his conversion in the autumn of 1820 through daily prayer and reading the Bible. He knew few Baptists but agreed with their views. He preached his first sermon in the Nanchunty church on February 10, 1821, at the age of twenty.

Soon he was licensed to preach without his knowledge, for his plans were to be a lawyer. Still he preached often in the nearby churches and in his father's home. Large crowds attended these services of the young convert and many made profession of Christian faith.

Howell then entered Columbian College in the nation's capital by means of financial support of friends, although his purpose still was to become a lawyer. After some eighteen months—which was the extent of his formal higher education—he withdrew without explanation from Columbian.

En route home from Washington, He was diverted by an advisor

in Richmond to engage in missionary work in the Portsmouth
Association. After seven months he became interim pastor and then
permanent pastor of the Cumberland Street church in Norfolk. He
was now, in 1827, in his twenty-sixth year. For transportation as a
missionary in Portsmouth Association he had bought a sulky and a
horse. Howell married Mary Ann Morton Toy, a member of his
congregation, in April, 1829. She was the daughter of a seaman and
of the matron of a hospital. Bride and groom moved into her
mother's quarters.

Restless to Go West

In Norfolk Howell developed a restless ambition to respond to the
continuing call of the Southwest, as did many settled pastors along
the Eastern Seaboard. He read the many articles appearing at the
time in the religious press about the spiritual dearth of the Great
Valley. The clincher came in two letters received in the spring of
1834. The first was an inquiry from the pulpit committee of the
Nashville church. The second was a commission from the American
Baptist Home Mission Society to serve in Nashville as a missionary
at an annual salary of $500.

There was a third coincidental circumstance which Howell seemed
never to connect with the other two. A man with a lifelong obses-
sion for note keeping, Howell left a still extant "private memoran-
dum," "Reasons for Resigning the Church in Cumberland Street,"
dated Norfolk, May, 1834: "I was on 17th of April, 1834, reelected
pastor of the church in Cumberland Street. The whole number of
the members 304. Number voting against me 18. I have declined
accepting the church for the following reasons: Divided into parties.
Critical of pastor for using notes, not interesting, exceeds authority,
favors individuals, will not give out hymns. Resulted in prostitution
of morals, sin, evils cherished by members."

Evidently the sensitive young preacher could not tolerate the
critical sniping of displeased members. The call to Nashville was
abetted by the gentle push from Norfolk.

Doubly motivated, positively but also negatively, Howell at thirty-
three in the summer of 1834 made the long journey from Norfolk

to Nashville (alluded to in the previous chapter). Strangely, this meticulous notekeeper left no log of the journey to visit a prospective field of service. The psychology of that lapse is in the abstraction of his thought processes. Not given to practical considerations, he was often absorbed with theological and philosophical thoughts.

Another Virginian, the witty Joseph Walker, pastor in Charlottesville, does record a journey in 1846 from Virginia to Iowa. He conducted four ladies and two children from Charlottesville to Dubuque—by water the entire journey except for one day by railroad and a single day's jaunt by coach to the final destination. Walker's engaging and often humorous "Notes on Travel" were published in the *Religious Herald.* The log: by coach down to Richmond, by riverboat on the James to the Chesapeake, by steamer up the bay, by train from Baltimore to Harrisburg, again by boat up the river to the foothills, and then in a canal packet by a series of lifts up and then down the mountainside, after which the trip was by river down the noisy Juanita, the flowing Ohio and up the proud Father of Waters past the treacherous shoals and the busy wharfs at St. Louis. Not until their last boat docked at Davenport did the jovial but weary Walker conduct his charges by the slow moving coach on the plains of Iowa. A summary of these "Notes" in the next chapter gives an example of travel at the time, one that much of the way was a parallel to Howell's journey.

In any event R. B. C. Howell made his eventful trip ten years earlier, all the way of the northern route from Norfolk to Nashville. Arrival from Cumberland Street in Norfolk to the City of Rocks on the Cumberland in Tennessee was in July, 1834. He visited six weeks in Nashville, preaching five or six times a week in the town of 6,000 and in the neighboring communities. In these services there were sixteen converts. The church in Nashville called Howell to be pastor on August 19, 1834. He accepted and announced plans to depart in two weeks to move his family.

Many years later, Howell would write what he called "A Memorial to the First Baptist Church of Nashville." This was probably in the summer of 1862 while he as a Confederate sympathizer was in a

Federal prison with three other Nashville pastors. It is still extant
in Howell's original handwriting, preserved by his descendants.
Typewritten copies were made in 1942 under the direction of
Prince E. Burroughs. In this he said that Nashville then had a population of "about 6,000, a flourishing university, a female academy,
many other excellent schools. As a centre of influence it has not its
equal then or now [1862] in the whole South West."

The philosophical young theologue leaves not a note of the homeward journey. But in Norfolk he tells a saddened congregation of his
plans to migrate to the West. The departure had to be delayed for
the birth of a third child—Morton, who made his appearance on
October 2, 1834. Then the plans were completed to sail from Norfolk. They could not take the usual route through D. C., Wheeling,
and the Ohio and Cumberland rivers because that was free territory.
Howell's mother-in-law, Mrs. Toy, still lived with them and would
until her death in 1859. She owned five slaves, which she hired out
as her only source of income. The party would not risk the strong
threats of fanatic abolitionists to the slaves. So parents, three small
boys (one an infant a month old), mother-in-law, and five colored
persons (three girls and two boys) made the long and hazardous
journey down the coast line, around the tip of Florida and across
the Gulf. It was a stormy eighteen-day voyage, but at New Orleans
they were still many river miles from journey's end. Finally the
family was greeted at the dock in Nashville on Saturday, January 2,
1835.

Ready for the Task

With his family housed at once in the hospitable Union Hall,
owned and managed by J. H. Marshall, Howell was ready for the
first Sunday's services on January 3. He was also ready with copy
for the first issue of *The Baptist* which appeared that same month,
its purpose "to unite, harmonize, and invigorate the Church in this
state." The design was to promote the "operations of Bible, Missionary, Tract, Education, Temperance and other benevolent societies." All brethren, wrote the editor, both "effort and antieffort"
were offered the use of *The Baptist* which was determined to avoid

all controversy. *The Baptist,* the first periodical of the denomination west of the mountains and south of the Ohio, would not be a
"party paper." There had been "strife and division enough," said
the editor as he invited all "to express their views freely," although
he "believed firmly in the United Baptist cause."

Howell's tenure as editor continued until 1846 when J. R. Graves
became an associate and for two more years, until 1848 when
Graves became sole editor. Both as pastor in Nashville and as editor,
Howell quickly became the Baptist spokesman for the entire region.
He visited associations and churches throughout the state. He was
a favorite speaker at college commencements: at the University of
Nashville (later Peabody), at Georgetown in Kentucky, in Louisiana,
and back at Columbian College. When Columbian conferred on him
the honorary Master's degree in 1837, the exercises were attended
by President Van Buren and other officials of state.

Howell had turned down many calls to other pastorates and to
college presidencies. It, therefore, surprised his Nashville congregation when in 1850 he acceded to the importunity of the Second
Church in Richmond, Virginia, where he was the immediate successor to Professor J. L. Reynolds and later successor to Joseph
Walker. It was while pastor in Richmond that Howell was elected
president of the Southern Baptist Convention, succeeding the first
presiding office, William Bullein Johnson. This was in 1851, again
in 1853, a third time in 1855, and again in 1857.

By 1857 Howell had returned to the Nashville pastorate, the
primary reason almost certainly being to combat the inroads of
Landmarkism. Under the influence of J. R. Graves, that movement posed about the most serious threat ever known to the existence of the Southern Baptist Convention. The reelection of Howell
as Convention president at the 1859 session in Richmond became
the issue for Southern Baptists. Graves was there with his organized
forces. Howell, too, had impressive strength.

A full account of the Graves-Howell controversy would fill more
than this volume. Summary justice to the historic event will claim
attention in succeeding chapters. Meantime it is in order to assert
the measured comment that this controversy was the most divisive

in all the annals of Southern Baptist life. Also, even now it can be
reported that Howell was reelected in Richmond on the first ballot,
by a narrow margin, and that he resigned immediately, declining to
serve on the ground that local problems should be settled locally
on the site of the debate. There were then four more ballots before
the Convention elected a president to take the chair as successor to
Howell.

Already we have Howell back in Nashville for his second term as
pastor. With his usual vigor he assumed the leadership in the church
and in the region. But the most enervating experience of an eventful
lifetime still clouded his horizon. The forces that divided Baptists,
and Methodists, and Presbyterians pointed to the inevitable civil conflict.

When war came, its devastation inevitably engulfed the border
state of Tennessee and its fair capital on the Cumberland. Nashville
fell to Federal forces on a Sunday in February, 1862. Sunday services were disrupted even while Howell attempted to preach. Finally
he gave up the effort, but he would not heed the advice of friends
who tried to persuade him to join the fleeing throng. By coach, on
horseback, by wagon, on foot, they fled the doomed city before the
Federals' approach from Donelson. But Howell stayed with his
people—that is, with those who were unable to flee, the elderly, the
women, the young.

A Stubborn Southerner

At length, he and other preacher suspects were thrown into prison
by the military governor, Andrew Johnson. Their freedom was offered on condition of taking an Oath of Allegiance. This no one of
them would do. Howell said: "I will rot in a Federal prison before
I take the Oath of Allegiance."

Before noting the reason for Howell's refusal, an observation is
called for. Howell, of course, was an opinionated Southerner. His
views were in line with those of other Baptist leaders in the South.
Richard Fuller had defended slavery in his extended debate by correspondence with Francis Wayland. Isaac Taylor Tichenor, in a Fast
Day sermon before the General Assembly of the State of Alabama,

said that "God was right when He instituted slavery among men; that it is the best form of human society, that it consists with the true happiness of both master and servant." Howell preached a sermon on the family in 1860 which was published in a Nashville newspaper in which he said that the family had ever been and would always be composed of three classes: parents, children, and servants.

In spite of this viewpoint, Howell's refusal to take the oath came on other grounds. A fellow Mason interceded with Andrew Johnson and brought word that the governor was surprised that Howell had not personally requested release. Only then did the pastor address a note to the governor explaining his determination not to take the oath. To take such a formal expression of allegiance, said Howell, would imply that he had been disloyal. That he insisted he had never been and so he would not by taking the oath imply that he had been disloyal. Immediately Howell was released to return to his people—but not to his pulpit for the Federal Army was using as a hospital the beautiful structure erected at a cost of $27,000 under Howell's leadership, 1836-1841.

Imprisonment had taken its toll. Sickness while in jail had rendered Howell too weak for transport behind the enemy lines. War itself drug a weary way for more than three years. By now Howell's strenuous years were well beyond threescore.

After war's end, the Southern Convention resumed its meeing, in Russellville, Kentucky, in 1866, the first session since 1863. Howell was again elected vice-president. He had held that office or the presidency at each session of the Convention's existence, except the ones in 1859 when he resigned and in 1863 when he was not present. At the closing session in Russellville the venerable old warrior, again a vice-president, pronounced the final benediction. It was the last time his voice was heard in the sessions with which he had been officially associated since the beginning.

The next January Howell had his first stroke. Realizing that he would not recover and being unwilling to be a hindrance to the progress of the church, he resigned in March, 1867. The fatal stroke came on a Sunday, April 5, 1868.

"I Close the Book"

A summary of his career this prolific notekeeper has himself penned. He recorded in his own distinctive longhand in his Pastor's Book:

"Here sadly, but as I trust resignedly, I close my Pastor's Book, I presume finally. I have been a pastor, without a single day's intermission, forty-two years and a half, nine years in Norfolk, Virginia; then sixteen years in this city; then seven years in Richmond, Virginia. I then returned and have been a pastor here ten years and a half. I was a licentate about five years before I was ordained, most of which time I was at college, and a missionary of the Association of Virginia. I have therefore been a minister forty-seven years and six months. I may, as I trust, be able physically to state briefly, the details of my labors and successes during this period. If I am not, most of them may be learned from a volume of forty-one manuscript notes of Annual Pastoral discourses which I have lately had bound.

"While pastor of the Church in Cumberland Street, Norfolk, Virginia, I baptized into the fellowship of that church, including those I baptized in contiguous places, in Hampton, in Elizabeth City County, in York County, in Matthews, in Norfolk County, in Suffolk, and in Elizabeth City in North Carolina, five hundred and ninety persons, of whom seven afterwards became ministers. I was also engaged with other pastors in the organization of four churches and in the ordination of five ministers of the gospel.

"While pastor of the Second Church in Richmond, Virginia, I baptized into the fellowship of that church, including some in Williamsburg, two hundred and seven persons; assisted in the organization of five churches and in the ordination of seven ministers of the gospel. In Norfolk I married ninety-nine couples and one hundred and seventy-four couples in Richmond.

"In Nashville I have labored first and last twenty-seven years and six months. During this period I have baptized into the fellowship of the First Baptist Church in this, including those baptized in the vicinity, especially in Franklin, Williamson County, in Murfreesborough in Rutherford County, and in Shelbyville, Bedford County, five hundred and fifty-seven, twenty-four of whom have become ministers; and I have assisted in the organization of six churches, and in the ordination of twelve ministers of the gospel. I have here united in marriage two hundred and sixty-four couples.

"By an examination of these numbers it will be seen that in the course of my pastorship I have baptized eleven hundred and forty-four persons which is an average of about thirty a year; that among those baptized by me thirty-one have become ministers, and I rejoice to find not a few of them occupying positions of usefulness and honor unsurpassed by those of any other ministers in our country; that I have assisted in the organization of fifteen churches, some of which are now very large and prosperous; in the ordination of twenty-four ministers of the gospel, and I have married five hundred and forty couples, and I have preached about nine thousand three hundred and eight sermons, seven hundred and eighty as a licentate and eight thousand four hundred and twenty-eight as a pastor. How many funeral sermons I have preached I do not know, having kept no definite account, but I suppose about a hundred annually, which would be forty-six hundred and fifty. Sermonizing has been with me a passion from my youth. These outlines will give some idea of my ministerial and pastoral labors proper.

"In the department of literature I have labored assiduously. These labors I have performed at intervals occupied by others in sleep, or in relaxation from toil, and without infringing at all upon my duties as a pastor. In January, 1835, I originated The Baptist in this city, which I edited without any pecuniary compensation for thirteen years, and a part of that time was also assistant editor of another paper, The Baptist Advocate, published in Cincinnati. At that time there was not a single Baptist paper but mine, south of the Ohio river and west of the mountains. This paper had a numerous list of subscribers, circulated in all the Southern Valley states, and was a powerful instrument for good to our cause. I have written and published about thirty pamphlets of different sizes, and six volumes on various subjects; and I have four others in manuscript now ready for the press. My published sermons, orations, reviews, and elaborate newspaper articles would make probably two or three additional volumes.

"I have reason to be profoundly grateful to my brethren every-where for the confidence and respect with which, both at home and abroad from the very beginning of my ministry, they have honored me. By their contributions my church in Norfolk made me a Life Member of the American Bible Society, the American Baptist Tract Society—now the American Baptist Publication So-ciety—and the General Association of Virginia. Subsequently my church here made me a Life Director of the American and Foreign Bible Society, and still later, and without my knowledge of when they did so, a Life Member of the Revision Assion (sic). On my assuming the pastorship in Cumberland Street I was elected clerk of the Portsmouth Association of which that church was a mem-ber. After two years, young as I was, and large and able as was that body, I was elected its moderator, to which office I was annually elected while I remained in Virginia. I was invariably also a member of the Board of the General Association of that state. I was also a vice president of the Triennial Convention for sixteen years, and until the organization of the Southern Baptist Convention.

"On my removal to Nashville I was elected president of the Baptist State Convention of Tennessee, and two years afterwards of the Convention of Western Baptists held in Cincinnati; took part in the organization of the Western Baptist Education Society which resulted in the theological institution of Covington of whose Board I was for many years a member. On the organization of the General Association of Tennessee I was elected the moderator and by annual elections continued in that position for thirteen years, or until I left the state and returned to Virginia. On the organiza-tion of the Southern Baptist Convention I was made one of the vice presidents. I remained in this position for four years, while meetings were designed to be triennial. I was elected president and the meetings were made biennial. I was president for eight years consecutively, having presided at Nashville, Baltimore, Mont-gomery, and Louisville. At Richmond I was elected for two years more, and declined to serve, and Dr. Fuller was elected. I was for many years presiding officer of the Foreign Mission Board and afterwards a vice president up to the commencement of the war of the Bible Board. At the next meeting of the Convention after that at which I declined the presidency I was again elected one of the vice presidents, and was regularly afterwards at each meeting reelected until after I was disabled by paralysis at Memphis in May last. This meeting I was unable to attend. Thus it will be seen that in the United States, in which I was in the beginning, and am now one of the vice presidents of the American Baptist Historical Society, as I was at the Triennial Convention; in the West, in the whole South; in Virginia and in Tennessee and in the District Associations with which the churches of my charge were connected—the Portsmouth in Virginia and the Concord in Tennessee, in which first and last I presided in sixteen annual sessions—the partiality of my brethren has placed me in the most prominent and responsible positions in the denomination of which I have been an humble but sincere member.

"On Lord's Day the 30th of December last I preached my fortieth—which was really my forty-first—Annual Pastoral Discourse. At the regular time in January—the Second Sunday—I preached and administered the Lord's Supper. After the sermon and preliminary to the Ordinance, I received by the usual forms into the fellowship of the church sixteen new members. I thought I then saw the beginning of a revival of religion among my people, which has since been justified in the immense numbers who have since professed religion in connection with all the various churches in the city and neighborhood. On Friday of that week—January the 11th—I was attacked by paralysis of the whole of the left side by which though I suffered no acute pain I was rendered utterly helpless and unable to speak plainly or to think consecutively. Not a few of my friends who had been similarly attacked had died, and I supposed that in my case the usual result would follow in a few days at most. I confess that I greatly preferred not to survive my ability to preach and labor otherwise in the cause of Christ. I was probably stupefied to some extent."

The account further details how he came to realize that his precarious health would not permit a continuation of an active ministry. Rather than be a burden or a hindrance to the church, he, therefore, resigned on March 15, 1867, the resignation being "dictated to a member of my family." The church appointed a committee, which finally recommended acceptance of the resignation, which action was taken on May 9, to be effective on July 1, 1867. On that date, Howell wrote, he "ceased to have any connection whatsoever with the pastorship of the church he had first served thirty-two years earlier.

The old soldier lingered nearly a year longer, dying on Sunday, April 5, 1868. He was buried on a hill in Nashville's Mt. Olivet Cemetery.

The credentials for being the subject of this study of the development of the Southern Baptist Convention are impressive

Vice-president of the Convention in its first years
President for a longer period of time and perhaps in more formative years than was the tenure even of its first president
Vice-president again after his resignation as president
Vice-president earlier of the Triennial Convention
President of the Tennessee State Baptist Convention and of the Western Baptist Convention
President of the Bible Board, the Foreign Mission Board, and of the Southern Baptist Publication Society
Moderator of Portsmouth and of Concord Baptist Associations
Clerk of the Portsmouth Association

Howell was elected to office in every Baptist body of which he was ever a member, and to every level of official responsibility. These positions of trust he held continuously from the first year of his mature career to the very last of his active ministry. These positions he occupied over the span of years in which the Southern Baptist Convention was coming into being. The sum of these varied experiences is the total which amply justifies the focus here upon the career of R. B. C. Howell as central to the early development of the Southern Baptist Convention.

Specifically, he was in the strategic position and at the given moment to fulfill the crucial need in denominational polity. That he met that need without a quaver is the happy report on these pages.

Profile of Howell

3

How They Got There

There was no overland road from Norfolk to Nashville in 1834. Morton Howell in his personal memoirs says that the preferred route which his father took on his visit that summer was by Washington and Wheeling—by water most of the way and by stage where no river or canal transportation was available.

Ever bent on his spiritual mission, R. B. C. Howell left no account of the mundane experiences of travel. Joseph Walker, keenly sensitive to the human factor, covered much of the same ground in 1846 which he reported to the *Religious Herald* in Notes of Travel. This was Walker's journey conducting a family of his congregation from Charlottesville to Iowa, most of the entire sixteen hundred miles by water. Walker's Notes give insight into the rigors of travel encountered by Howell on the long jaunt from Norfolk to Nashville in the summer of 1834.

Three Ways of Travel

Three principal modes of travel then posed a choice between as many evils. There is no agreement as to which constituted the least disagreeable of the three tortuous devices of man by which he removed from one locality to another.

There was the coach—the jolting, straight-seated, dusty-in-dry-weather, leaky-in-wet-weather, cold-in-winter-time Concord drawn by six high-spirited steeds urged on by an adventurous driver anxious to deliver in record time the President's inaugural message or other important papers. A dozen to a score of bruised passengers were jammed inside and stacked on top, their luggage wedged be-

neath and behind the seats. The vehicle was hurried over rough
roads, around curves and up mountain defiles by the straining
animals at the breakneck speed (for a Concord coach) of ten miles
an hour.

There were the cars on iron rails which at times hurtled awe-
struck passengers along the countryside at the dizzy pace of fifteen
miles an hour, meantime hurling cinders in their eyes through open
windows, covering them with smoke, and shaking them unmercifully, as with dexterity they held the hard, straight seats. There
had been little development of railroads in the agricultural South,
which was a matter of small moment to Southern planters who
preferred, if it could be had, travel by water.

So there was the boat—the coastwise steamer plying along the
Atlantic and between Gulf ports, the river vessel of varying sizes
and degrees both of safety and physical appointments, and—oddity
of all oddities in travel accommodations a hundred and fifty years
ago—the canal packet!

Indeed, canal travel was regarded as the cheapest and the safest
of all means of going places in the first half of the last century. The
canal packet was the preferred vessel moving along the artificial
waterways. A flat-bottomed, stub-nosed boat accommodating a
hundred and fifty passengers, the packet was pulled by livestock
driven along the banks of the four-foot deep water, the boat moving
night and day at a speed of from three to three and a half miles
an hour.

Nighttime witnessed an amazing adaptation for sleeping in two
of the three cabins on the packet. Shelves were drawn out from
the walls, three deckers, each just barely high enough above the
lower one to allow a medium-sized person to crawl in. In the men's
cabin forty-two berths were thus made ready. A little bit of straw
enclosed within muslin and facetiously called a mattress and a pil-
low of similar construction afforded the only cushioning on the
boards. At least half of the passengers slept (or tossed and tumbled)
on tables (the same on which they had eaten their meals during the
day) and on the floor. Under such circumstances men usually
crawled into their berths or stretched out in their assigned spot

without removing their clothes, and the man was regarded a sissy
on a canal packet who took off more than his shoes and coat at
night. Those garments which were removed were hung on a common line running the length of the cabin.

When this change of scenery was effected, a weird drama in the
darkness was enacted as seventy-five to a hundred men tried to
sleep (two to a berth). The long night hours were filled with grum-
blings and groanings and tossing of the men, punctuated occasion-
ally by a stentorian snore as one of the number found brief surcease
in fitful slumber.

During the night no doubt more than one would attempt to es-
cape, thinking the night air on top the boat would be heavenly com-
pared with the stuffiness around his hard berth. Most likely as he
attempted to clamber down, his foot would strike the line of clothes
or some warm shoulder on a spot which had been vacant when he
retired. Reprimanded in no uncertain terms by the owner of the
shoulder, he would retreat to his shelf, there to remain, breathing
softly, until welcome morning, if the underpinnings did not give
way under his berth to bring him toppling down on the poor fellow
beneath.

A similar arrangement in the ladies' cabin accommodated the
women and children. The crew slept in the remaining cabin in the
bow of the boat.

These were the three modes of travel a century and a half ago—
coach, train, and boat—all crude and painfully slow. In addition, of
course, there was much private travel by horseback and wagon, but
men got about chiefly by these public means of transportation.

From Charlottesville, Virginia, to Dubuque, Iowa Territory, was
a three weeks' journey for Joseph Walker and his friends. It was
a trip—this crossing of the populated eastern side of the continent—
slowly negotiated by boat fifteen hundred of the sixteen hundred
miles. Even the mountains, from Harrisburg to Pittsburgh, were
crossed via Pennsylvania's famous canal system, this two hundred
and fifty mile leg of the journey normally requiring three days and
three nights for an average speed of three and a half miles per hour.
The time was comparatively short, however, to travelers with an ap-

preciation for the aesthetic, for nature put on her most attractive attire in the Alleghenies.

Joseph Walker, when he left the parsonage at Charlottesville, on a bright morning in July, 1846, was departing on no between-Sunday trip. Twenty-seven days passed before he reached his destination in Dubuque, a week of which had been consumed in Norfolk loading baggage, selling furniture, and arranging for passage for the "four ladies and two children" whom he was escorting to Iowa Territory, whence they were going to join relatives.

By coach Walker and his party rode down to Richmond the first day; thence on the James River they boated the next day to Norfolk. When a week had passed, Pastor Walker and his friends embarked by steamer for Baltimore. From Baltimore to Harrisburg, capital of Pennsylvania, was the only section of the journey traversed by train, the cars following the winding Susquehanna River on a hundred-mile run which required ten hours. The rest of the journey all the way to Iowa was by boat—by natural and artificial streams to Pittsburgh, down to Cincinnati, past Louisville, down the broad Ohio to Cairo, and then up the Father of Waters to St. Louis, a busy river town of several thousand hardy westerners.

At Davenport, the "first commercial point" in Iowa Territory, Walker's party left the "Uncle Toby" because they "did not receive that gentlemanly treatment from her Captain, clerk, and some of the servants, which is due the traveller." The letter-writing pastor felt that it was a merciful Providence which provided a convenient vehicle (coach) for the remaining sixy-five miles of the journey.

Babies, House Guests, and Cholera

When R. B. C. Howell visited Nashville in August, 1834, in response to the invitation of the Nashville pulpit committee, he probably followed essentially the same water course as did Joseph Walker. At Smithland, on the mouth of the Cumberland, he may have transferred from the Ohio to a Cumberland riverboat for Nashville. Or in the event of the Cumberland being too low for river travel he could have taken a stagecoach, at Smithland or earlier up the Ohio.

Later, when he moved his family, passage was on the packet
"Ajax" out of Norfolk—a six-weeks' voyage to New Orleans. Leaving Norfolk around the first of November, the family arrived in
New Orleans about the middle of December. Still before them was
a two weeks' river trip, up the Mississippi, the Ohio, and the Cumberland. Morton Howell was a month old when the family left
Norfolk. The family included two other boys, each under five years
old, plus the young parents; Mrs. Howell's mother and her five
slaves—three white adults, two colored adults, three colored teeners,
and three baby boys.

The family was welcomed at the Nashville wharf on January 2,
1835. They were lodged in Union Hall, a hotel on Market Street,
later known as the St. Charles Hotel. Howell rented a house on
Summer Street and Cumberland Alley in which the family lived
until 1843 when the pastor built a brick residence on Summer and
Deadrick. Lots had been bought for $1,918.50 on which the resi-
dence of three floors was erected. Mrs. Toy, the mother-in-law,
had her room in the basement where were also the kitchen, dining
room, and servant's room. A parlor and study were on the main
floor. The floor plan and architect's perspective have been preserved in the family archives. The contractor for the sturdy structure was George W. Burton.

Baptist pastors passing through Nashville, according to Morton,
always stayed in the Howell home. This clipping from *The Baptist*
for August 29, 1846, is in Morton's memoirs: "The Southern mail
coach brought to our door and we joyfully received our beloved
brethren Shuck and Yong." The two, J. Lewis Shuck and the
Chinese native Yong, had attended the meeting of the Southern
Baptist Convention in Richmond the previous June.

Another visitor from Portland, Maine, stayed six months. He
had come one morning before dawn. Morton also tells about Professor Cyrus Smith of Murfreesboro writing "to Miss Dorinda Law-
son of New York to meet him at my father's house in Nashville
and marry him." She did as instructed, stayed in the Howell home,
the two were married on October 7, 1841. Neither of the bridal

pair, says Morton, was an acquaintance.

Missionary Shuck and the Chinese convert also stayed for several days. Crowds thronged the home to see and hear Yong, a Chinese Christian in the flesh. One evening the crowd filled the street.

In 1848 the community heard that cholera was coming. "We knew that everyone would die," Morton Howell wrote. The disease appeared in January, 1849. By June the epidemic prevailed generally; it ceased about July 1. Morton thought that it spread from the cool water of the springs—Nashville then had no public water system. He saw many wagons and carriages of people fleeing from the scourge. Morton's sister "had cholera but she did not die."

The cholera epidemic which hit Nashville that year caused adjournment of the triennial meeting of the Southern Baptist Convention. Fear of the disease restrained messengers from coming to the scheduled sessions in Nashville. Only twenty-eight braved the reported plague. R. B. C. Howell, as a vice-president, called the meeting to order. President William B. Johnson had written that he would not be present and recommended that the session be held in Charleston, South Carolina. This the small band in Nashville decided to do, and the official 1849 meeting of the Convention was held later that same month in Charleston.

Steamboat navigation on the Cumberland, according to the *History of Nashville* edited by J. Wooldridge, had its "rise, reign, and decline within one generation." The first steamboat from New Orleans arrived in Nashville in 1818. Citizens formed the Nashville Steamboat Company which built in Nashville some river vessels. Luxury boats were called "magnificent floating palaces." The twelve-hundred mile round trip from Nashville to New Orleans was made in three weeks. The record from port to port of five days and eighteen hours made by the "Nashville" before the war, Wooldridge says, probably never was beaten.

Louisville and northern stages arrived and departed daily in Nashville. There were daily departures on the three and a half-day run to Memphis, daily to Huntsville, three times a week to Clarksville. Strangely, many of the lines departed at 11 p.m. or even 1 a.m. Passengers would apply at the hack line for passage, register, and pay in advance for a seat. If there was an overload, those who had been the first to register had the preference, and those remaining had the preference for the next day or the next week.

Turnpikes were built by private companies. The Lebanon Turnpike Company was incorporated in 1836. A thirty-mile macadam road, Nashville to Lebanon, with tollgates at either end, was built at a cost of $240,000. Some other turnpikes out of Nashville were Buena Vista, Granny White, Brick Church, Nolensville, Hillsboro, Franklin, and Hyde's Ferry.

Wooldridge reports the Lexington and Ohio Rail Road as having been begun on October 22, 1831. The first railroad in Tennessee, from Nashville to Chattanooga, was opened in 1854.

An Editor's Frequent Journeys

In 1845 William Carey Crane came to Nashville to be associated with R. B. C. Howell on *The Baptist* and as professor at Union University in Murfreesboro. Soon, however, the restless Crane—native of Virginia, formerly pastor in Montgomery—was preaching in Columbus, Mississippi. Now only thirty-seven years old and full of energy—as well as alert to the human situation—Crane continued as associate to Howell on *The Baptist.* He also took three months to answer the call of the Columbus church. With the pastoral duties he combined his editorial work in Nashville.

Thus Crane made frequent journeys by coach from Nashville to Columbus, to which there are occasional references in his editorial releases. (It is also appropriate to note that Crane was almost certainly courting again. His first wife had survived only ten years after their marriage, his second only sixteen months. Howell reports in *The Baptist* Crane's third marriage to Catherine Jane Shepherd of Mobile, but Crane himself never breathes a word in his columns about it. Maternal mortality in those days was high. It was not at all uncommon for a man to be married several times because of the ravages of childbirth.)

When Crane wrote on "The Beauties of Stage Travel" it could have been with tongue in cheek. One suspects some note of sarcasm in this account   in *The Baptist* from 1844:

"Stage traveling is sufficiently agreeable on the route here [Nashville to Columbus] as far as Mt. Pleasant. . . . The president elect [Polk] whom we had heard speak one week before emerged from his own mansion, as our stage passed, as if to do us greater honor, and bowed to his acquaintances among our fellow passengers.

"But when the mud road commenced, then came the rubs, the jolts, the pitches, and all the beautiful contortions incident to an easily swinging coach. Night comes, and before it concludes its darkness, we are most unmercifully laid flat upon our side on the roadside, with a forehead bearing scars of dishonorable contact, with the upright of the stage door.

"Good reader, pardon us, for alluding gayly and with a cheerful heart to an upset of a stage coach. Our fellow passengers, Mr. Thomas, the stage Agent, and an intelligent young lady, who so honors us, as to choose us for a traveling companion to Florence, were only stunned, and our own head simply bruised. Thanks to some sturdy Tennesseans, we were soon all set to rights and going ahead. . . .

"We dined in Florence with the friends of our accomplished traveling companion, Miss D. Leaving Tuscumbia, we first broke the coupling pin, and then the braces. Now we were riding upon a rail, and anon were stayed up in the stage, by an overgrown sapling.

"By walking and riding we made out to go about ten miles in six hours. Then we transferred all our baggage to an open wagon and in this primitive conveyance, two of us holding pinewood knots, flaming high with pitchy light and dripping exquisitely refined tar, we travelled on, until the clouds began to discharge their contents upon us.

"Then darkness reigned, mud felt peculiarly soft under wagon tracks, and corduroy roads made us exceedingly prepared for an early breakfast, which it was not our fortune to obtain. The light of a new day dawned upon us in the vicinity of Russellville.

"From R. on to this place we noted little to vary our feelings of the scenery. We passed through barren regions, we saw towering pines, we marked the line of Buttahatcha river, we followed with a bird's eye view the range of hills which turns off the waters on the one side into the Tennessee river and on the other side into the Tombigbee river. Big Bear Creek and Little Bear Creek hills were as steep, as rocky, as savage looking as ever. . . .

"Though raining hard, and partially soaked, as both inside and outside passengers were, our coach safely landed us at the Blewett House on Friday in the afternoon, following our departure from Nashville. Our blood tingles yet more freely in our fingers from all our exposure. C."

The following April Crane made a boat trip from Columbus to Mobile which he reported in the columns of *The Baptist.* He left Columbus on Monday, April 21, by the steamer "Potomac." On the return he left Mobile on Saturday, April 26, and reached Columbus on Tuesday, April 29. The account is doubly remarkable, first for its glimpse of riverboat travel but even more so for its omission of the event in Mobile on April 23 which occasioned the journey.

Here is what Crane wrote for *The Baptist,* in an article titled "Ourself":

"The trip was very agreeable and quite rapid. Mobile at this season is very pleasant, strawberries were quite abundant; flowers in wild profusion; vegetables in plenty, and ice creams, and all the concomitants of 'ice,' to one's heart's content. . . . The places of public resort have a wild luxury, which is greatly dissipating. . . .

"We came back in the elegant steamer 'New Era.' Well officered, well provided, and in fine style of furniture, and with a sumptuous table. These creature comforts one needs much on a long steamboat trip. We were compelled to travel on Sabbath, accordingly at the request of the officers and passengers we preached in the afternoon (while the boat was under full press of steam) to the passengers, over 200 of whom were on board. . . . Our friends will see that (*we*) made a mistake by heading this article *ourself."*

The inference of that last sentence is Crane's only indication that the journey was a wedding trip. One must learn from other sources that he was married in Mobile to Miss Shepherd on April 23.

Crane was the son of a prominent merchant in Baltimore. He had been educated in his native Virginia and in New York where he met and married both his first and his second wife. At thirty-seven he had been pastor in Virginia, in Baltimore, and in Montgomery. His uncle, James C. Crane, was a secretary of the Southern Baptist Convention, to which office the younger Crane succeeded and continued as secretary for twelve years. According to Cathcart's *Encyclopedia,* Crane later declined the presidency of five male colleges and six female colleges, before assuming successively the executive leadership of three others in Mississippi, of Mount Lebanon University in Louisiana, and then in 1863 of Baylor University in Independence, Texas. He also became president in succession of three state Baptist conventions, Mississippi, Louisiana, and Texas. A much travelled and able and influential denominational man was he.

Reports of missionary labors published in *The Baptist* listed one missionary as being appointed for four months at $15 a month. Another in six months of service had ridden 500 miles and preached 50 sermons. Another in 91 days rode 754 miles, preached 160 times, baptized one, and was paid $60. S. Love was paid $60 for 120 days, travelled 1200 miles, baptized six, conducted the Lord's Supper twice, attended 24 church meetings, visited 800 families.

Unwearied Benevolence

"Notes of a Tour by Dr. Babcock" (Corresponding Secretary of the American and Foreign Bible Society), published in *The Baptist* for December 21, 1844, afford another glimpse of missionary travel in Howell's time. En route from Kentucky to Round Lick church near Lebanon in Tennessee, Babcock was joined at Hopkinsville by "our beloved yoke-fellow, Rev. J. M. Peck on his way from Illinois to the General Association of Tennessee."

Early in the afternoon of his second day on the road, Babcock had reached Hopkinsville. "A little after midnight," he wrote, "we boarded an over-filled stage, and quietly seated on the top, took up our line of march. Long before sunrise we had passed the southern boundary of Kentucky and for the first time in our lives entered her neighbor Tennessee. Breakfasting in Clarksville. The whole of this

day's ride was unusually slow and wearisome, through a country
less interesting than we have usually found in the West and over
roads which to say the least, do no credit to the public spirit or
private enterprise of the inhabitants.

"Half tired to death we reached Nashville at a late hour. Have
our readers either gentle or simple, ever made the transition from
such a coach, at the end of such a day's ride, to the luxury of a
first rate hotel, such as we found kept by our excellent brother,
J. H. Marshall, and deservedly regarded as the headquarters of both
travellers and boarders who desire quiet, neatness, comfort, and
good fare, at reasonable charges, in this proud capital of the state?

"The next morning in company with our valued correspondent
and friend, Dr. Howell and several brethren, we took our line of
March to Wilson County.

A few miles out of Nashville on the macadamized Lebanon
turnpike—which Babcock said greatly contributed to the ease of
travel in contrast to the roads of the previous day—they stopped
at the Hermitage to see the former president, Andrew Jackson.
At the door the servant told them that the master of the house was
sick, whereupon the ministers declared their intention to continue
without disturbing General Jackson. But Old Hickory, learning
who was at the door, would have none of it. He urged them to
come on in, insisted that he was eager for their fellowship, engaged
with them for an hour in animated conversation about their forthcoming meeting at Round Lick.

The following June Editor Howell wrote: "I have this hour
[Tuesday evening 10th June] returned from the funeral of General
Jackson. . . . We knew General Jackson well, much better privately than publicly. In the bosom of his family he . . . mingled
with a gentleness and affection we have never seen expressed. . . .
The service was conducted by Dr. Edgar of this city. . . . We
were particularly pleased with the detail given by the preacher, who
was with him at the time of the General's Christian experience,
when, about six years ago, after a whole night spent in agony and
prayer, under the influence of the most pungent conviction, the
love of God was, at about daybreak, shed abroad in his soul, and

he was filled with joy and peace, in believing. The very next day he united with the church" (the Presbyterian in Nashville).

Back in December, after the Hermitage interlude, the Baptist messengers continued their journey, the ride that day terminating in Lebanon. The next morning they were on their way to Round Lick church near Three Forks, less than two miles from the turnpike. "The Round Lick edifice," wrote Babcock, "is in a beautiful grove. Nearby flows the stream from the union of Three Forks, a picturesque view which a painter would admire. For nearly half a mile the horses, carriages, and vehicles of different descriptions gave indication of the extensive gathering [to hear J. M. Peck].

"On adjournment, we proceeded to the place assigned us for quarters—some two or three miles distant—where a very large number of guests soon assembled. Had not our kind entertainers possessed an unusual amount of genuine, unwearied benevolence, their patience would have been exhausted. For four days not less than thirty of us were accommodated in an ordinary sized house, filling the table three times in succession at each meal, and comfortably lodging some dozen or fifteen in a room. . . .

"After supper each night, these guests, together with the family and servants of our host—making up a congregation of some fifty souls—attended religious services; a sermon or two being delivered on each occasion by some of the ministers present."

The Baptist, of October 26, 1845, reported the Tenth Anniversary of the General Association of Tennessee Baptists, a meeting held at New Hope on Thursday. Meetings were on Friday, Saturday, and Monday. The delegation was back in Nashville on Tuesday. Sunday they attended church services. Six nights—Wednesday through Monday—there were guests in homes. At this meeting R. B. C. Howell was named "a delegate to attend the Southern Baptist Convention to be held next Spring in Richmond."

Continuing his Sketches of South West Tour, Babcock wrote in *The Baptist* (Feb. 1, 1845): "Readers will little care for our personal adventures and endurances in these few days; nor are we inclined to lionize ourselves by the enumeration of petty incidents of drenching rain and mud through which our horseback excursion led;

or the perils of our misdirected 'way in the woods,' leading us many
miles aside from our appointment, and the haste of a most killing
effort to reach it in season."

The traveling agent described Nashville as being "situated on the
south bank of the Cumberland river, more than 200 miles from its
mouth, it is easily reached by numerous steamboats which regularly
ply between this and almost every important place on the western
waters. The site is undulating and rocky, with elevations varying
from 50 to 175 feet above the river's bed. It is interspersed with
beautiful cedar groves, and the environs are justly said to 'present
the richest variety of landscape scenery'; the river seems to meander
where it should, and the evergreen hills have the proper elevation
and position to give boldness and symmetry to the picture; in short,
it is altogether one of the most romantic, healthy, and flourishing
little cities in the valley of the Mississippi. Its present population
is probably ten or twelve thousand and is increasing in a healthful
and pleasant way, not by shoals of incongruous immigrants rushing
in to give it a motley and unharmonious character, but by its own
natural product of homogenous materials.

"The public buildings are numerous and creditable to the state;
and when the lofty acropolis, a square containing four or five acres,
more elevated than any other portion of the city, which was pur-
chased last winter by individual subscriptions [actually, by the city]
and given to the State—shall be crowned with the contemplated
state capitol edifice, there will be nothing wanting in the complete-
ness and beauty of the whole appearance.

"Midway on our course (to McCrory's Creek) we overtook and
passed a quiet old gentleman, also on horseback, dressed in gray
home-spun cloth, with saddlebags and overcoat mailed on behind
him. Our young friend and guide suddenly reined up his horse, and
looking over his shoulder, exclaimed, "Yes, it is, it is father Whitsitt!'
The good old gentleman was on the way to meet our appointment.
By previous information we were prepared to appreciate his worth,
and our rare privilege in thus unexpectedly meeting him. The remaining miles of our ride seemed too short, and we gleaned not a
little pleasure and profit from his interesting and instructive conver-

sation."

The rider was James Whitsitt, pioneer Baptist minister who had helped the Nashville congregation reorganize after most members had gone into the Campbell movement.

Babcock cites these statistics: missionary Baptists of Tennessee (in 1844), 19 associations, 360 churches, 226 ordained and 61 licensed ministers, 25, 431 members; anti-mission Baptists, 26 associations, 367 churches, 179 ordained and 19 licensed ministers, 13,824 members. There was said to be a much larger proportion of the latter to the former in Tennessee than in any other state.

Howell wrote an article on the State of the Church in Tennessee, in response to which a man named Jesse Cox wrote to complain that the editor was a stranger in the state and, therefore, could not be informed as to the true conditions. He objected especially to Howell's assertion that the progress of the churches was backward, insisting that the churches in the South and Southwest were enjoying perfect peace both in faith and practice. Progress, he said, was steady but slow.

In defense of his qualifications to write on the State of the Church, Howell pointed out that he had traveled from Mississippi to Virginia the past twelve months (his first year in Nashville). He had read most of the associational minutes. He had engaged constantly in much correspondence, with as many as a hundred currently, all by longhand. He had valid information. He was not a "foreigner."

Howell named as deliberate policy in his role of denominational service the two practices of visiting the churches and associations and of maintaining his wide correspondence. His means of travel were by coach, on horseback, by buggy, and by water.

4

Look, What He Found

The unsettled state of religion which Howell found in the South-west simply beggars description. No one word known to Webster is adequate. Religious views of the widest difference marked the times. These views were expressed with utmost candor. Debate was the order of the day. To these debates between popular champions the people flocked in great numbers and with unabated interest. Lines of the sharpest distinction were thus drawn between the denominations.

In Nashville, for instance, Baptists were late in getting started. Their tardiness played to the advantage of more punctual denominations. Presbyterians were ahead of the Baptists, and Methodists were so far in advance that by the time Howell came on the scene he said that Methodists outnumbered the Baptists by five to one.

It is altogether possible that in that period of such sharp dispro-portion the followers of Wesley looked down their noses at these upstart Baptists. At any rate, the editor of *The Christian Advocate,* Methodism's official organ, leveled his editorial guns directly at the editor of *The Baptist.* The attack was repulsed, of course, with vigor.

Ere long Howell's associate, the always controversial J. R. Graves, entered the fray. The upshot was the appearance of Graves's famed appraisal of Methodism, *The Great Iron Wheel.* In reply to Graves, a raucous-voiced layman and politician named Brownlow, who later became governor of Tennessee, wrote a 300-page book *The Great Iron Wheel Examined.*

The Meaning Was Clear

A man defended his position, in plainspoken language. He also told his personal opinions without reservations and in print. Some typical excerpts:

James Whitsitt, writing in *The Baptist* (1835):

"The Tennessee Baptists never will be right, until their doctrine and practice agree. . . . When they come to mind the things of Jesus Christ more than they do their own things, their practice and doctrine will agree."

Of two debaters (1844): "Each abounds in self-esteem, a necessary quality for such occasions, and each is skilful in extricating himself from difficulties in which his assurance has involved him."

From *The Tennessee Baptist* (1844): "Imposters—We find the following in the *Knoxville Register* of October 16: Beware of the Swindler. We learn that an individual calling himself John H. Slack, is now in town, and endeavoring to make it appear that he is authorized to solicit donations for a College in Washington, D. C. His name and general appearance correspond with those of a person who has frequently been advertised in several Northern papers as an imposter. We understand that his course after leaving this place will be towards Nashville and New Orleans. We perform our duty to the public by putting them on their guard against him."

In the *Biblical Recorder* was this notice: "An Imposter. The Church at Ramoth Gilead, Pasquotank county, North Carolina, cautions the public against a man by the name of Bedford, who has been expelled by said church for immoral conduct, and who still has in his possession a license to preach, granted him some time prior to his apostacy. Agreeably to the latest intelligence, the said Bedford was traveling and preaching in the Western part of the State [N. C.] having with him a woman who passes as his wife—his true wife having been deserted, and left in the county aforesaid. It is hoped that the churches in this State and in Tennessee whither it is said he is wending his way, will be on their guard against this vagrant imposter."

"Withdrawal of Fellowship. Whereas Elder William H. Hughart has, to the great detriment of the peace and harmony of the churches composing this Association, been promulgating the peculiar

views of Mr. Alexander Campbell. And, Whereas the said Hughart,
after the expression of the diapprobation of this Association of his
views, both at its last and its present session, did on the 22d of
September, 1844 in the town of Buchanan, where there is a regular
Baptist Church and while this Association was in session, proceed
to constitute his followers into a church—Therefore,

"Resolved, That this Association disclaim all Christian fellowship
with the said Wm. H. Hughart, and declare that he is no longer
viewed, by us, as a Baptist minister; and that we hereby affectionately warn the churches and individual members against him, as a
zealous propagator of error and proselyter to his erroneous views—
operating all he can on the weak and unstable.

"Resolved, that the Clerk be requested to forward the above preamble and resolution to the *Religious Herald* for publication.

C. Tyree, Clerk of the Valley Association"

Such plain speech was not designed to cultivate brotherly love.
Indeed, fellowship was then evidently less valued than honest
opinion. It was certainly secondary to doctrinal integrity.

Divided on Missions

Doctrinal soundness was regarded as a superlative virtue. And
doctrine revolved around the continuing clash between the divine
sovereignty of Calvinism and the free will of Arminianism. The issue
came to focus on the question of missions. It was the same authoritarian viewpoint expressed earlier in England by the old conservative
preacher who had said to the fervent William Carey after he had
preached his famed missionary sermon: "Young man, when God
gets ready to save the heathen, He won't need you to help him!"

In the Southwest, the antimissions spirit had been preached up
and down the hills and valleys by a man named Daniel Parker. A
favorite tale about Parker went the rounds in Howell's day. Some-
one asked Elder Parker if he made a contribution after Luther Rice
had made an appeal for foreign missions. Parker replied that he
had no counterfeit half dollars. If he had, he would have thrown
in, but as he had none he would not throw away good money for
such an object.

The Baptist reported some associations as passing resolutions of nonfellowship with churches that supported mission societies. One read: "We hereby declare that Bible, Tract, Mission Societies, and the Sunday School Union, are inimical to the peace and harmony of the churches. Therefore we will not TOLERATE any member, in membership, in any of the above named Societies" (Peter S. Gayle letter, *The Baptist,* Jan., 1835).

One church expelled two members, each of them a preacher, for attending the meeting of a mission society. The two then gathered around them others of like sentiments who organized a "United" Baptist church, which prospered immediately, while the church that expelled them dwindled away.

Division of this kind which was said to be prevalent often resulted in two associations of the same name as well as pairs of churches existing side by side occupying the same territory, each claiming to be the true and orderly body.

Baptists were designated as United or Regular, Separate or Particular, Effort or Anti-effort, sometimes as Missions or Anti-missions. Generally, Howell concluded, there were two classes, Predestinarian and Arminian. The extraordinary revival at the beginning of the century, he said, had projected a discussion of Divine Sovereignty with attendant heart burnings, agitations, and conflicts that continued for years. Predestinarianism and Arminianism formed the staple of almost every discussion.

Gradually, he said, and at last irremediably the contestants were thrown asunder. First the verbal trysts cooled their feelings toward one another, then alienated, then embittered. These controversies found their way into associations. When malignancy became intolerable, compromise might be formally adopted only to be observed by no one. Division of the churches resulted throughout the whole country with concomitant evils.

Predestinarian churches became known as United Baptists and Arminian as Separate Baptists. They felt for each other, Howell says, "probably less charity than for their neighbors of the Pedobaptist churches."

In consequence of the current agitations, Howell wrote in sum-

mary that resolutions were passed by churches and associations
against the Tennessee Convention and similar organizations. Frequently, also, these resolutions opposed Sunday schools, Bible
societies, Education societies, Temperance societies. It was asserted that such were unauthorized by the Word of God, were condemned by the true principles of religion, an innovation upon
Baptist practices, and the development of Arminianism (as opposed
to Calvinism). They were said to be monied institutions, corrupt,
and corrupting of character. All such organizations, the recurring
resolutions charged, ought to be suppressed, and the faithful
should resolutely practice nonfellowship with all who supported
them. There was scarcely a church in all the state, said Howell,
into which such resolutions had not found their way.

Invariably proponents discussed their treasured statements with
fiery temper, driving away religious feelings. If possible an early
vote was forced. If the statement was adopted, friends of missions were expelled. If not, the opposers of missions declared
themselves to be the "orthodox and orderly Church."

When they could, Howell said that the antimissions forces
seized the records and the meetinghouses (as Howell well knew
from the painful experience of his own congregation). The same
scene was reenacted at associations. Or if not, a new association
was organized. Thus resulted the side-by-side churches and associations, divided on the nagging question of effort or antieffort,
of society or antisociety.

Sitting on the Whirlwind

In the first issue of *The Baptist,* for January, 1835, the editor
wrote of the "disordered state of the church throughout a large
portion of this commonwealth and most other parts of the great
valley of the West." In anticipation of his task as editor of a religious paper in this setting he concluded that "the prevalence of
intestine discussions, the conflict of opinion on doctrinal as well
as practical religion, and the operation of perhaps many other
causes equally disturbing will we apprehend render the task of conducting a religious periodical at the present crisis extremely

arduous."

He admitted that the church itself, to which he had come as pastor, was enough "to occupy all our powers." Yet he felt impelled "to sit upon the whirlwind and manage the storm which now rages in the moral world." In attempting to do so, he said that "we tremble that we should not be able to accomplish all the good which it is desirable *The Baptist* should effect. . . . We may aid in quieting the jarring elements of discord." There were, he noted, "many faithful pious and talented laborers already in the same work with ourselves."

Howell pledged to respect other denominations, while being "a firm supporter of the principles of the word of God as held by the Baptist church, known in this city and state as the United Baptist Church." He added that "the editor holds these principles deliberately under a solemn conviction." He promised to "seek their dissemination while deprecating the most distant approach to sectarian exclusiveness and guarding most rigidly against the spirit of partisan rivalry with his brethren of a different faith."

Columns of *The Baptist* would report ordinations, constitution of churches, proceedings of associations and conventions. Thus he would "preserve a record, build up the walls of Zion, avoid controversy, let contention alone." "If we gain a conquest at all," he added, "it shall be a victory of love."

Pleading both with "effort" and "anti-effort" brethren to engage together in the same labors of love," he said that many publications were needed for "Western Virginia, North Carolina, South Carolina, Georgia, Alabama (west of the mountains), the whole of Mississippi, and many other portions of the great valley." He was confident that from all of these areas the people "will turn in this direction for religious intelligence."

Howell's first issue printed the minutes of the West Tennessee Association which met at Gray's Bend on the Duck River in October, 1834. It was noted with regret that the work was on the decline, the fifteen churches reporting a net loss of 15 in a total membership of 513. Peter S. Gayle, who as a missionary of the American Baptist Home Mission Society, had preceded Howell in Nashville, wrote to the editor that churches throughout most of the state "are extremely unsettled." There were in the state he said "about thirty thousand communicants." Gayle also complained of a trend toward making associations ecclesiastical courts "to regulate and bind the consciences of the brethren." It was Gayle who in the same letter gave the example of the association that went on record that "Bible, Tract, Mission Societies and the Sunday School Union are inimical to the peace and harmony of the churches" and resolved to have no fellowship with churches that tolerated members who belonged to such societies.

In that first issue *The Baptist* reported the ordination of one Lemuel Hall Bethel at Spring Hill in Gibson County. At the annual meeting of the Sweet Water Association, in September, 1834, there were reported 207 baptisms; 2,085 members; and 2 new churches. One John Cobbs had left his wife and children to go to Missouri with another woman and was now imposing himself as a minister.

The Tennessee Association met in Knox County at Mount Pleasant Church: 28 churches, baptized 372, total members 3,483. The constitution of the East Tennessee Association indicated that its participants were "United Baptist churches," that "no officer or manager was compensated for services."

Why They Differed

One explanation offered by Howell for the complexity and multiplicity of doctrine was that most of the population were first-generation settlers from all points beyond the mountains. The preponderance of the new population had, of course, pressed directly through the mountain passes of the Carolinas and Virginia, but a surprising number had drifted down from Pennsylvania, New York, and New England. J. R. Graves, for instance, the intense controversialist of the following decades, was from Vermont, as was also his partner A. C. Dayton, and the third of their troublesome triumvirate, J. M. Pendleton, had migrated from Pennsylvania first to Kentucky and then to Tennessee.

These from their many backgrounds brought with them their native customs, practices, and beliefs. Two significant aspects of that variety of background in its effect on the new synthesis of culture in the Great Valley need to be borne in mind.

First, social and ideological differences as related to geographical distance were much more pronounced at that time than would be true now. Distance apart then was much greater because of the relative difficulty of communication. There was then no immediate communication through the modern media marvels that have become commonplace to our urbane civilization. The coming of the mail—often called "recent intelligence"—was a community event awaited with sharpest expectation. The telephone had not then even been invented, and radio and television were so far in the future as never to be the projection of the wildest imagination.

Thus, the psychological and emotional differences of those who settled the Valley, though they may have come from localities to us today seemingly not greatly distant were as if they had originated far, far apart. When they settled together in the developing new country, it was to bring about the amalgamation of many sharp dissimilarities. It is really no wonder, then, that there were resultant tensions. These differences were most pronounced in religion.

The measure of miles apart was much greater than now—greater in thought patterns, in life-styles, in fundamental practices and customs. Two families, even though they were from adjacent counties, might therefore be very much foreign to each other.

Second, this very sharpness of background was the basis for a sometimes unconscious cultivation of suspicion and mistrust. Prejudices could be pronounced, as is evidenced in Howell's own snide intimations about "foreigners," northerners, and fanatic abolitionists. Indeed, one can feel the deprecating tone in his editorial reference to a certain missionary as being "from England" and to another "from the North."

Characteristically, the frontier spirit developed a tenacious independence. The heterogenous population brought their heterogenous views, and they held to them with determined persistence. This independence, along with other factors, formented the rabid opposition to "Societies," "conventions," "boards"—indeed to

all forms of controlling organizations. Especially vocal was the
frontier opposition to any banding together of religious forces.

Campbell's Peculiar Views

A single specific instance from Howell's own early Nashville
experience may provide the best general understanding of the overall
scene he confronted in 1835. Of course, it is naive to imply that any
one particular embraces or portrays the whole. The state of religion
and the culture of the times are too complex to admit of a simple
explanation or of one single satisfactory example.

But still a look at the church in Nashville and of the inroads
Campbellism had made upon it will be instructive. Earlier, James
Whitsitt of Mill Creek and others had been concerned to get Baptist work going in Nashville. By the 1820's a church was under
way—small, with irregular services, often uncertain as to available
pastoral leadership.

When the church was looking for a pastor in 1826, there was in
the congregation a young schoolteacher, Phillip S. Fall, who was
also a preacher. Of course they had him to preach. Of course they
were delighted with this bright young man, one of their own number. Of course they implored him to become their pastor. A couple
of years before, when he was then teaching in Kentucky, he had
steadfastly declined their call.

But now the call was made official, and he accepted. This, although some knew that in Kentucky their young pastor had shown
some inclination toward the "peculiar views of Alexander Campbell."

At this point it is well to remember that the two Campbells themselves, father and son, had been Baptists after the father's separation
from the Presbyterians. It was not their intent to form another denomination from their growing and zealous following in western
Pennsylvania and western Virginia, where they lived. Rather, they
concentrated their efforts even more in the middle portion of Kentucky and Tennessee. They strongly preferred to refer to their
movement as "the reformation." The purpose was to "reform"
the Baptist and the Presbyterian churches, especially at the points

of church government and church ordinances.

In his illuminating book, *Men Who Made the Churches,* Paul Hutchinson establishes the valid point that the Campbell movement brought into being one of the very few distinctively American-born religious bodies, now known as the Disciples of Christ. In their beginning they were "sons and daughters of America's first frontier." They were "as American as the buckskin jacket" in that "storied period when the long emigrant trains began to find their way over the Appalachians, down the Ohio, and on into the prairies of the Middle West."

That frontier, writes Hutchinson, was "a strange conglomeration of hard living and religious fervor," marked by barreled whiskey, the filthy village inn, dueling, and low moral standards of a young population which was hot-tempered, self-willed, individualistic.

With all the vices, Hutchinson avers, there was "a never-flagging interest in religion." In every community lines were clearly drawn, everyone knowing where each stood, whether bound for heaven or for hell. The circuit rider and the wandering evangelist always commanded a following, with religious discussion prevailing before, during and after the camp meeting which became "the social center of the sprawling countryside."

On this sprawling scene Thomas Campbell, a Scotch-Presbyterian, coming by way of Ireland, made his appearance in western Pennsylvania in 1807. His "Declaration and Address," an appeal for Christian unity, he wrote in 1811. Alexander added his slogan: "Where the Scriptures speak, we speak; where the Scriptures are silent, we are silent." Their doctrine of reform in their own inclusive literalism the Campbells proclaimed near and far. Although Alexander led his church to withdraw from the Baptists in 1830 and adopt the name of Disciples, the more readily identifiable historical term at the time is Campbellism. It was then a most pronounced influence in the religious community, especially in the middle region of Kentucky and Tennessee.

Campbellism was rife in the whole area: it was present in some measure in all the churches, and it was in fact a lively branch from the Baptist tree. No real cause for alarm, then, that the young schoolteacher-pastor had been casually impressed by "the reformation." But before long it became apparent that Pastor Fall's adherence was more than a slight impression. He was not going through young growing pains that would soon disappear.

Preaching from the pulpit Sunday after Sunday was increasingly imbued with Campbellism. In a short time the pastor gained more and more followers from his own congregation, as would be expected. The ultimate—and expected—result was that almost the entire congregation followed the pastor into "the reformation." Only a few of the members remained steadfast to the traditional Baptist position. The majority finally assumed that they were indeed *the* church. They took the church records, they took the church building, they took almost the entire congregation. The pastor who led them away served the congregation for many years.

With the emotional support of men like James Whitsitt of Mill Creek the little discouraged band held together. They experienced some growth under somewhat uncertain leadership. In the summer of 1834, the still very small congregation, through its pulpit committee, wrote the historic inquiry to Robert Boyte Crawford Howell, pastor in Cumberland Street of Norfolk. He responded with his visit and then to their call to be pastor. In truth the challenge of need in Nashville was typical of the destitution in the Great Valley as Howell undertook his arduous task in 1835.

The Progress Is Backward

In summary, Howell wrote a two-thousand word analysis for his paper which he called "The Church in Tennessee."

"The progress of every portion of the Church in this state, "he asserted, "is backward. The standard of religion is low. Restlessness and discontent are prominent. The dark picture is relieved only by two or three instances of revival in Eastern and Western districts and in some two or three churches in middle Tennessee."

In this dismal condition, he wondered, would "the effervescence of the mass dash asunder its bonds and destroy itself" or would it "only work off its impurities."

5

Toward Concert of Action

The imperative demand in any community enterprise is to achieve cordial cooperation. Such can never be achieved by decree, by edict, by legislation, or even by logic. The appeal that wins approval is to the heart, for sincerity of commitment issues from deep feelings rather than from the intellect.

The independent spirit of the times—no more than one generation removed from the raw frontier—accented the necessity of cordiality in cooperation on the part of Baptists in the South in 1845.

In a perceptive student's evaluation of Howell's career, Rufus B. Spain asserted in the *Tennessee Historical Society Quarterly* (1955) that Howell determined to a great extent the development of the Baptist denomination after 1835. "He led a disunited and retarded frontier denomination," Spain wrote, "in the acceptance of a unified and progressive program of education, cooperative missions, Sunday schools, temperance, and denominational unity when these were unpopular in the West."

R. B. C. Howell's earnest conviction of the need for unity he expressed as early as the second issue of *The Baptist* in February, 1835. In union, he wrote, there is strength. "Conquering armies are formed of individuals acting in concert."

Baptists in Tennessee, he said, were dilatory at the point of uniting their efforts to preach the gospel to every creature. At a time when "heresies of every description are rife and rampant," he was convinced that the most serious heresy was the persistent unwillingness to work together. This pulling apart rather than together, this "turmoil and strife have desecrated the fairest portions of our Zion." In consequence, there was "a barrenness, not of bread but of the Word of the Lord in all our land."

Howell was also very clear in what he meant by acting in concert. "This agreement," he patiently explained, "this union, this concert is a missionary association." Individuals formed a society, churches pooled their energies in an association, churches and societies appointed representatives to form conventions. Concert of action pointed inerrantly to associations, conventions, boards, and institutions.

Chiding those who opposed such combinations, Howell inquired: "Why are brethren grieved for our engaging in missionary effort? This effort is not unorthodox in doctrine. It is not immoral. Why then do anti-effort brethren talk of withdrawing from us? We ask no one to do what he is not convinced is according to the will of God. We interfere with no church or association regulation. Will they exclude our brethren because they feel it their duty to labor for the spread of the Gospel and the salvation of souls?"

How Many? How Far?

These comments reveal the sequence of feeling both of the proponents and of the enemies of concert of action. Concert required the formation of organized bodies to elicit, combine and direct committed effort. Both friends and enemies raised two fundamental questions: How many? How far? Friends said that organization should comprehend both the number and the degree of responsibility commensurate with efficiency. Foes said that the number should be nil or at least no more than the church itself (or the local congregation); the nature of the assignment to the organized body must never violate the autonomy of the church.

Right here in these two questions was the battle joined with regard to concert of action.

The relevance of the two questions—How many? and How far?— is readily illustrated by friends and foes alike. For instance, R. B. C. Howell himself was named in 1846 to a special committee of the Southern Baptist Convention to consider the need for a board for

"Bible and Publication." The committee recommendation (Howell himself, remember, being a member): "Resolved, That this Convention does not deem it advisable to embarrass itself with any enterprise for the publication and sale of books." The committee recommended that Bible distribution be done through the Foreign and Domestic boards.

The Arguments Stated

The nature and intensity of opposition to the proposed "concert of action" were expressed by Jesse Cox in his letter to the editor of *The Baptist* referred to in Chapter III (*The Baptist*, May, 1835). Cox insisted that the "present disturbance in Middle Tennessee" was due to the influence of "foreign ministers." These had come into the state from afar teaching "something in faith and practice" to which the people were not accustomed, thus causing disturbance. It is clear that Cox means by "something in faith and practice" setting up associations and conventions.

"We claim to be predestinarians and missionaries," Cox hastens to add, "but not according to the system of the present day, but according to the ancient missionaries."

Cox insisted that some of his party preached as constantly as those under the patronage of the Convention, but the accounts of their preaching were not published in the religious periodicals. He said he had examined the reports for six or eight years, and the more he examined the more he was "opposed to the general course pursued." Many Convention proposals he admitted were "good in themselves, but the manner was unscriptural."

"You say," Cox continued, "that the church is the highest tribunal. Agreed. Why then form one of a lower order to do what is her duty. Or of her members form a society? I dare not state that the churches or her ministers have done all their duty to spread the gospel, but this is no excuse or pretext for having done what the New Testament does not authorize. As bad to do what we are not commanded as not to do what we are commanded, or if we do not do it according to directions. I believe it is the duty of ministers to preach and of churches to sustain them. The manner is plainly laid down in the New Testament."

Warming to his own argument, Cox proclaimed that benevolent societies are "an amalgamation of the church and the world." He said he had no objection to these societies in their proper place, but that proper place was not in the church. Churches that had promoted the organization of societies "had gone beyond what the New Testament has directed." Their course had caused opposition such as Cox himself was expressing.

"If they will return to the directions given us," Cox argued, "there will be peace. They have the power to make peace without sacrifice. We have not. We cannot leave the New Testament. We ask that you remain and be at peace."

Howell replied that "the design of the Convention is simple." It is a united labor "in this state to spread the Gospel. God has sent them [missionaries], and we sustain them. Brother Cox objects only to the manner. The church as a whole is bound for the ministry as a whole, in Arkansas or New Orleans, as much bound as in any other place.

"His contention is that it is wrong for good men to agree to do right. They pass resolutions in churches, in conventions, in associations to excommunicate. Never do we. We seat them. We do not withdraw fellowship."

Will Baptists Ever Unite?

In a sad commentary, Howell summarized in his Memorial the standard resolutions of opponents of organizations which they offered in churches and associations against conventions and similar organizations. Frequently these were also against Sunday schools, Bible societies, education societies, temperance societies "as unauthorized by the Word of God, condemned by the true principles of religion, innovations upon Baptist practices, development of Arminianism, monied institutions, corrupt and corrupting of character."

All such societies, the resolutions invariably averred, ought to be suppressed, and Christians should resolutely declare nonfellowship with all who supported them. All very much alike, there was scarcely a church in all the state, said Howell, into which such resolutions did not find their way.

When resolutions opposing societies and other such organizations were offered, whether in churches, associations, or conventions, they were discussed with fiery temper, driving away religious feeling. Proponents of the resolutions forced an early vote. If the resolutions were adopted, as they frequently were, friends of missions were expelled from churches, and churches were expelled from associations.

If the opposition to organization did not prevail, they would set up their own party within the church and declare themselves to be the orthodox and orderly church. When they could, they seized the church records and the meeting house, as Campbell's followers had done in Nashville prior to the coming of Howell.

Similar scenes were reenacted in associational meetings. Churches were expelled from associations on the same grounds as individuals were expelled from churches. If the opposition could not muster the strength to expel churches for supporting concert of action, they organized a new association covering the same geographical ground.

Howell had come to a church which had experienced this kind of separation prior to his coming. His church was plagued again in the same way in 1838. In that year the followers of one Washington Lowe adopted this resolution: "The majority of the First Baptist Church in Nashville, having joined the State Convention for missionary purposes, and involved themselves in other like so-called benevolent institutions, have departed from the faith, and practice of the Gospel, and are now in heresy, and disorder, and therefore no longer a church of Christ; that we the minority, having maintained the faith, and preserved the order of the gospel, are truly and legitimately the church; therefore we are the true and only First Baptist Church in Nashville; and claim to be so received and accepted."

The separated group called Washington Lowe, and he accepted the pastorate. The next month the First Church erased from its roll those who had formed the new body.

With pathos in his tired voice Howell later asked: "Will the Baptists of Tennessee ever be united and labor together continuously in the cause of Christ? Scarcely did they recover from one division when they fell into another. Would to God this had been the last!"

Since he was now writing in retrospect, Howell knew that the answer to his deep longing was not to be affirmative. Therefore, he had to add with a sigh: "But alas yet another awaited us, still more destructive!" Through his long career, this kingdom warrior had on his worn hands the battle with opponents of concert of action.

A view which was to become very familiar, but then as now indefinite in execution, was proposed by John Bond of Wilson County writing in *The Baptist* in June 1835: Let each church contribute funds, keep its own records, and report to the association. When the church keeps "her own work in her own hands, as Jesus commanded," then Bond concluded joyfully there would be "no need for the State convention." Just how the church was to do this Bond did not make clear—perhaps because he had not thought that far.

Associations Must Not Rule

But on one point there was clarity and agreement: The proposed concert must not abridge the autonomy of the churches. An association should never become an ecclesiastical court. The denominational body, whether an association or a convention, should not rule over the churches.

An early correspondent to *The Baptist* deplored a noticeable trend on the part of associations to dictate to the churches. Howell recurringly cited the constitution and by-laws of denominational bodies as pointedly denying any authority over the churches. He also designated these bodies as "mere missionary societies," always in a context refuting any argument that they were tribunals with doctrinal or administrative controls.

Extreme care was enjoined to make certain that concert of action, as needful as it was, should never infringe upon church government. This caution was clearly enjoined in response to each of the two fundamental questions. The number of boards (of organized bodies) should be kept at the minimum. The extent of responsibility should be carefully defined.

In a Letter to United Baptists in Middle Tennessee *(The Baptist,* February 1835)* John Blodgett expressed his "views on missionary enterprise on which you are unhappily divided." Agitation of feeling and difference of opinion, said Blodgett, "tend greatly to mar your peace and hinder your prosperity." For authority in missionary effort, he said that they must go directly to the Commission of Christ.

It is not treason against the church, he argued, for individuals to act and form conventions. No dictation or invasion of the rights of the church are involved. It is simply an agreement to obey Christ by sending the gospel to the destitute by those who contribute freely. By forming a convention they are enabled to do a work they could not otherwise do. The church standing alone, he argued, does not do it.

Supporting Blodgett's position, Howell agreed that churches, at this point, had always been dilatory. Therefore, he pled, "individuals must make up this lack of service on the part of the church. When the church, as such, shall come forward and do all that missionary associations, conventions, etc. now propose to do, these associations and conventions shall cease. The church has always lingered in regard to obeying this commandment" (of sending the gospel to the destitute).

"This Land Shall Be Thine!"

An example of the growing drive to achieve concert was the report of the Western Baptist Convention in its meeting in Cincinnati in November, 1834. Six states in the West were represented by 38 ministers as delegates. There were seven delegates from benevolent societies in the East, plus thirty or forty lay brethren. These were described in *The Baptist* of February, 1835, as "heralds of salvation, defenders of truth, amid the thickening multitudes that were settling that immense and fertile valley."

They met for six days. "All, or nearly all of the benevolent operations peculiar to the day were brought under view," according to the summary report. "Concerning some of them measures were adopted for their immediate advancement. Institutions already in existence—tract, Sabbath schools, Bible, temperance cause— were encouraged to greater and more united efforts. Materials were collected and adjusted for a few others either entirely new or hitherto imperfectly organized.

"The cause of Home Missions received a strong and well-directed impulse. Efficiency of effort of the American Baptist Home Mission Society, mainly directed to western states, will greatly depend upon the active cooperation of Western Baptists. Many churches destitute of one to break to them the bread of life will soon be supplied and new churches will be called into existence."

Delegates also called for support of Baptist Foreign Missions "to sustain a Baptist Mission to the great empire of China."

Baptists of the Mississippi Valley, the report concluded, "are rich but have never been called on to aid the cause." Enthused by the six days of the convention, the writer felt that the moral and religious prospects were decidely good, admittedly were not even fairly commenced. There were "ignorance, prejudice, an unsettled population, heresies, popery, and infidelity, under all the peculiarities of a new country." But in a moment of ecstatic inspiration, he reported that a missionary "in that great valley has lifted up his hands to heaven and exclaimed, 'Lord Jesus, this land shall be thine. The church will never give up the struggle till it is full of the knowledge of God.'

"What can restrain the influence of such men and such a spirit?" the writer expostulated in full confidence. "The West is safe if Christians do their duty—and they will. . . . That great valley shall yet be made as the garden of the Lord."

Moving Rapidly in All Directions

In a more subdued tone, Howell may have been less swayed by enthusiasm in his two-thousand-word analysis of The Church in Tennessee (*The Baptist*), March, 1835."Like an army without concert," he wrote, "the church moves rapidly in all directions. Will the effervescence of the mass dash asunder its bonds and destroy itself, or only work off its impurities!"

"It was the gloom of that scene that made Howell feel that the standard of religion was low, marked by restlessness and discontent." The dark picture, he had noted, was relieved only by two or three instances of revival in Eastern and Western districts and in some two or three churches in Middle Tennessee, including his own in Nashville. The prevailing disquiet he said was due to the "uncongeniality of the great whole." Perhaps it was a natural consequence of "a multitude from distant and remote points, each bringing peculiar habits of thought and modes of action from former residence."

Distinguishing "peculiarities of our ministry," he wrote, "are boldness, originality and vigor of thought, precipitancy in decision, confidence in the correctness of their conclusions, a singularly inveterate attachment each to his own peculiarities, a proneness to extremes, and an impatience of opposition."

These dissimilar backgrounds, Howell was certain, had given rise to many "strange and unheard of doctrines—such as 'the two seeds'—which has corrupted and laid waste many a pious heart." He also was convinced that these diverse and independent views had caused the associations to "assume a new character." Gradually they were assuming "legislative control, extending their authority as ecclesiastical courts." He was concerned that these evils should be removed and to bring about a restoration of union and harmony.

Howell saw that this aim could be cultivated by ministers coming together "once a year at some central point." They could "preach together, pray together, become acquainted personally at the State Convention." He also proposed correspondence by ministers through the columns of *The Baptist* and through other religious papers. Religious newspapers, he said, are among "the most efficient auxiliaries to the ministry of the Gospel."

The great need, John Blodgett declared in his Letter to United Baptists, was for unity of spirit. A wrong spirit he insisted prejudices judgment. Contentions hurt the cause. The object in concert of action is not to overcome one another, but to help one another "We are joint heirs," Blodgett wrote. "When one is injured, all are injured."

The plea of Blodgett, because of its underlying premise of organizations, fell on deaf ears in some resolute quarters. Lipscomb Norvell objected instantly to the appeal for missionary organizations. He contended that there were Christians "who are sincere workers" who disagree with Blodgett.

The need for unity of spirit, for a cordial concert of action, was illustrated in *The Baptist* by an article (May, 1835) contrasting the strong growth of Baptists in New York with their slow development in Kentucky. In twenty-three years Baptists in New York had trebled while in Kentucky they had only doubled, and that at a time of sweeping migration to the West. In New York the gospel was preached and churches planted along lakes and canals by missionaries of the Baptist Mission Society of Massachusetts. In Kentucky there was little cooperation to preach in destitute places.

In the Southern state the writer characterized the ministry as being marked by "rivalship, jealousy, ambition." "They have not pulled in an even yoke. Hence parties have been formed, divisions produced in associations, declarations of non-fellowship made, and frequent mutinies in the camp. This will always be where the ministry is independent of the churches and the true pastoral relation is not sustained."

Clinching his argument for unity, the writer asserted: "In New York let any Baptist minister 'set up for himself' and attempt to make his party and he will have the whole ministerial corps against him, backed by the churches. Not even could the strange and uncertain sound of a Campbell break the Baptist ranks in New York."

Where there is "unity of design and harmony of effort" the writer said that the cause will prosper. Without it there is defeat. This is the sure result of declaring "nonfellowship with friends of benevolent institutions," of excluding "brethren for becoming members of Temperance and Bible societies."

By thus separating themselves they promoted "a schism in the Baptist church." The writer concluded: "The effect of their opposition is seen in the condition of their churches. Such are the legitimate results of an illiberal, narrow-minded, covetous disposition. These men set themselves in opposition to the divine command to preach the gospel to every creature and urge others to adopt the same course. Their churches are decreasing and in a few years must become extinct. Their pulpit labors are not blessed, their congregations are dwindling away and God has evidently set the seal of his high displeasure on their proceedings."

Citing the record of one association as an example, he said: "Something is wrong in the system when twelve ministers labor for six months and only three persons are added to the churches under their preaching. This association will have to mend its ways, or else their place and habitation will be given to more faithful stewards."

The concert of action toward which there was perceptible movement involved churches making voluntary contributions to "sustain missionaries with food and raiment." It offered no interference with the independence of churches nor with the rights of members. As an example, the General Convention of Western Baptists was composed of "such brethren in regular standing in Baptist churches as choose to attend and cooperate with us." The business of the Convention—any Convention—is "to promote missions, ministerial education for those licensed by the churches, Sunday Schools, Religious periodicals, Tract and Temperance Societies, and all others warranted by Christ in the gospel."

In a moment of ecstasy a Sunday School missionary back from eighteen months in Mississippi wrote in *The Baptist* (April 9, 1835): "How excellent is thy convention in which the friends of Zion may concentrate their talents, their efforts, and their charitable contributions in the promotion of their Redeemer's kingdom at home and abroad. Under the influence of which . . . every latent emotion to do good may spring forth and bear fruit. . . . How excellent the spirit that devised such a praiseworthy combination of charitable enterprise in the West! And how magnaminous the effort that brought it forth! May the projectors and patrons long live to see the glory of the Lord triumphantly crown the work of their hands."

6

Toward Ministerial Improvement

Opportunities for formal education were limited in the Great Valley at midnineteenth century. Morton Howell in his unpublished Memoirs says that the despised "free schools" were attended only by the very poor, and that public schools (as distinguished from the "free") were established in 1853.

Meantime Morton himself was enrolled in several different private schools, each taught by a man who was a pedagogue as a means of livelihood. Two sessions were offered annually, from January to May and from July to December, with classes daily from nine till twelve and from two to five.

One of his teachers "was also a preacher who went back to Boston. There he preached and villified the people that had befriended him the six years he was in Nashville," Morton writes with unmistakable feeling. "At the beginning of the War he said my father ought to be hung as a rebel."

Morton's feelings about another teacher's incompetence also shows: "In January, 1846 [Morton was then fourteen] my father sent me to a man named Graves to a school on Spruce Street. A Vermont Yankee, [he was] totally unfit by both temperament and education to be a teacher. To his unfitness to teach I attribute my early antipathy to algebra and geometry. He knew nothing about math. The two sessions in this school I then considered and still think were time lost." One school that Morton attended in his tenth year was taught by a man named Davis "in the basement of the Cumberland Presbyterian Church."

Evidently a person could set up a private school without public controls as to training, experience, or qualification. Patronage was determined by the teacher's ability to persuade the public of his personal competence. J. R. Graves' own offer of his personal services to the Nashville community was stated by this notice in *The Baptist* (1845):

"The Rev. J. R. Graves of Lexington, Ky., has arrived in Nashville and wishes to conduct a classical School the next Session. He may be found at the City Hall."

One writer reported that in Ohio and Kentucky one-third of the children were "entirely destitute of education." Of Indiana's half million people only one-third of those under twenty-one could read. In Illinois it was said that "not one female in ten can read."

Sunday Schools, which historically had been started a generation earlier in England to teach poor children to read, were a definite ally in the learning process in the old Southwest. Morton notes that children were taught the alphabet in these Sabbath schools, which in his own church his father had initiated before the end of the first winter of his pastorate in Nashville. To Morton one of the most commendable features of the Sunday School was its library. There were he says "many little books, chiefly printed by the Society for the Diffusion of Useful Knowledge of London."

The proliferation of private academies illustrates further both the need and the limitation of an effective system of education. Over a span of twenty-five years, 1825-1850, many of the present Southern Baptist colleges had their origin—Richmond, Mercer, Howard, Judson, Furman, Wake Forest, Carson-Newman, Georgetown, Baylor, William Jewell, Mississippi College. Many academies—both male and female, and perhaps more of the later than of the former—sprang up everywhere, each inaugurated by a forceful personality with compelling vision.

With characteristic boldness and self-assurance, R. B. C. Howell addressed the obvious need for ministerial improvement. It may be that one provocation was a subconscious recognition of personal limitation. Never a man ready to admit personal limitations, it is quite certain that any such feeling on Howell's part, if indeed there was such, would have to be subconscious.

But the younger Howell makes clear the father's lack of formal training. He had learned reading, writing, and ciphering in "the old field schools." In his nominally Episcopalian family, he had read the Bible and the Book of Common prayer.

At the time of his conversion in his nineteenth year, Howell wanted to be a lawyer, but, Morton wrote, "he was doing nothing to that end." What he was doing, Morton did not know; "He was not going to school nor reading books for he had none."

In the next three years, in which time he was a fervent witness to his own family and community and was licensed to preach without his knowledge, R. B. C. Howell still pursued no schedule of private or formal study. When he did enter Columbian College at the age of twenty-three, it was for an incomplete tenure to be terminated suddenly and without explanation. Morton says that his father was in Columbian College a total of sixteen months and eleven days: "He did not graduate. He was not a student for a whole session anywhere."

And yet one of the editorial comments upon R. B. C. Howell's death in 1868 cited the fact of his well-known "proficiency in Hebrew, Greek and Latin," and that "more than eighty bound volumes of closely written sermons grace the shelves of his extensive library." Is it any wonder that one with his alert mind would be keenly sensitive to the need for what he called "ministerial improvement"? Militant crusaders often are activists in the very field of their own deprivation. Howell had little formal education, but paradoxically he was a well educated man, and he was a driving activist in a life-long crusade for the training of ministers.

Another general paradox is readily apparent to any reader of the literature of the times. Although formal training of ministers, whether general academic or theological, was scant, the facility with words of those who then had what we would call limited advantage is a marvel. Read for proof the letters to editors. Read the editorials. Read any extant literature of the times.

The culture of the times produced a superior quality of writing. The educational system may have been poor. Even that poor system may have been available on a limited time schedule. But the witness of what they wrote is unmistakable. Their writing then, on the average, was better than today. Better by far. The general public then simply expressed themselves better then than is commonly done today. They had a mastery of words, a facility for putting them together meaningfully, unknown today in our semiliterate culture.

Two comments are in order. First, they probably did have more time—or did they just take more time? Think of a man (R. B. C. Howell) carrying on an active correspondence with a hundred key persons all over the land—and doing so *in longhand!* Both the necessary time to do so, and the required physical care to do so *by hand,* demands an attention to words and sentence structure which are definitely compromised in a generation which would mechanize even thought processes.

Second, popular thought was addressed in sincerity to theological and philosophical pursuits. Howell commented that Calvinism and Arminianism were daily the topics of common discussion. One must surely gain some choice competence with words to be able to converse intelligibly about the theology of Arminius or the absolute divine sovereignty taught by John Calvin.

It may be even supportive of the implied effect of these two circumstances to insert here another comment about the characteristic daily activities of the preachers in those times. It was said that they "were mostly educated between the handles of a plow. There they have their study." Their usual classroom, it was said, was the cotton furrow and their theology they developed between the plow handles. Here, too, they had time to ponder the deep things. Even between the cotton rows or in grubbing hickory stumps a thoughtful man could formulate impressive doctrinal content.

Two of R. B. C. Howell's own brothers became Baptist preachers. One of them, Alfred Cogdell, "licentate," was received "by application" in the Baptist church in Nashville March 10, 1839 when he was thirty-one and dismissed by letter December 11, 1842. Of the other, Rigdon, Morton reports that his grandson said that he was "eloquent in prayer, but a sorry preacher." Rigdon was a man of "powerful physique." His first wife died shortly after the birth of a daughter, and he married a widow six weeks later.

Within his own family R. B. C. Howell perhaps realized the need for "ministerial improvement."

Full-Time Commitment

That improvement he contended should come about first of all by ministers themselves giving themselves wholly to the ministry. In "A Word to the Ministry" (*The Baptist*, June, 1835) Howell struck hard at the fallacy and ineffectiveness of part time-ministry.

The church, he wrote, is under authority to support the minister, but the minister is equally under authority to give his whole time. The whole church must support the whole ministry, a principle which was "universally admitted and universally disregarded." He charged ministers with refusing to give themselves wholly to prayer and the ministry of the word; in consequence, churches decline "the provision that they live of the gospel."

In an editorial of 3,000 words spread over three pages of fine print, the dead certain editor charged preachers with part-time commitment. By their own attitude they were responsible for church inertia in support of the ministry. The church, he wrote "has a horror of paying preachers" but it is a horror instilled by the ministry.

Many preachers, he had noted, point their sermons with keenest ridicule against ministerial support. With withering sarcasm they "preach against money, against salaries, against paying preachers." But let some member take a preacher behind a building or out in the woods and slip him a dollar or even two dollars. It is an instance of the congregation correcting the error of the pulpit. And what does the preacher do? He takes the money in violation of his own preaching.

When churches are properly taught, Howell insisted, "they will do their duty nobly." The people, he said, were generous and high-minded, honorable and benevolent. The soil, he added, "is luxuriant, the climate is salubrious, the markets convenient. With prudence, industry, and economy one can earn wealth." The people were not poor, nor did they cling to their gold. Baptists were simply not informed. It was an evil among Baptists, for the ministry of other denominations had no reason to complain.

All of this, Howell made clear, was to enforce his argument that the improvement in the ministry would come about primarily by a change of attitude, by a full commitment to the ministry. Churches would support a complete dedication to the ministry when the preachers were willing to give themselves fully to the ministry.

The Remedy Is Clear

Have ministers taught correct doctrine? he asked. "If not, the remedy is clear. Let them retrace their steps, give themselves wholly to prayer and the word, and teach the people."

Even the word "hireling" Howell used with approval. A term of reproach, especially in reference to ministers of other denominations, it was spoken sneeringly of those who stressed the duty of supporting the gospel. "Do not shrink from 'hireling,' " Howell counseled. "It was used by the Saviour and applied to His ministers. They are hirelings. They are hired by the church. They are hired to preach. Paul was a 'salary preacher.' "

Howell decried the limited view of the ministry and partial dedication to it of those who worked at their own business—"some of them get rich"—and neglected the flock whom they assumed to serve. Right here was the great need for ministerial improvement. In one summary sentence in his Memorial, Howell said that inferior ministers marked the times.

In January, 1845, as "comparatively an old man, in the ministry twenty-three years, a pastor eighteen years," Howell pled more earnestly to the churches: "You ought to have entirely the services of your Pastor. He should be required to live in your midst; preach to you, at your own house of worship, every Lord's Day; and visit, and hold prayer meetings, in your neighborhoods all the week.

"You have been satisfied with too little pastoral attention. The cause is suffering, and will, unless more is done, suffer irreparably. . . . This way of preaching but once a month, and performing almost no pastoral services, will starve out any church. . . . Some say that a preacher ought not to be paid. If he attends to his business and just goes and preaches on Sunday we agree. If a minister is really a pastor, he needs support and God requires that you give it."

To the pastors he spoke with equal earnestness: "Do not deceive the churches by promising to be the pastor and failing—fail you do, if you preach only once a month. Do not be reluctant to speak in the pulpit of pastoral support. Be frank and cordial about the annual allowance. Be more sedulous and constant in the performance of pastoral duties. Cultivate warm feelings of affection for all classes of men."

A New Era in Ministerial Education

Coincident with the meeting of the Western Baptist Convention in November, 1834, the Western Baptist Education Society had been organized. At the time of this organization meeting Howell was en route by sea with his family from Norfolk to Nashville, but even in his absence from Cincinnati the new Nashville pastor was made a director of the Education Society.

In the summary of his career which Howell penned as the last entry in his Pastor's Book, he said that two years after coming to Nashville he was made president of the Convention of Western Baptists and "took part in the organization of the Western Baptist Education Society which resulted in the theological institution of Covington of whose Board I was for many years a member."

The Western Convention in its 1834 session had taken measures to establish this seminary which ultimately came into being at Covington, Kentucky. The Society was charged with the task of determining its location, its character and general principles of instruction, appoint the trustees and instructors and fix their tenure, provided that each is a member of a Baptist church. The constitution of the General Convention of Western Baptists stated the business of the Convention to be to "promote missions, ministerial education for those licensed by the churches, Sunday schools, religious periodicals, Tract and Temperance Societies, and all others warranted by Christ in the gospel."

One of the delegates at the 1834 meeting of Western Baptists in

Cincinnati wrote that the "cause of education, especially ministerial education, awakened a still deeper interest" even than Foreign Missions. It was time he said "to give it a patient and faithful investigation" because of the "wants of a thoroughly educated ministry and the general destitution of the means of education in the west." This delegate left the Convention "with the full conviction that a new era in the cause of ministerial education had commenced in the West."

The same delegate reported on a resolution "to establish a Central Theological Seminary." An able and judicious committee, he wrote, was under appointment by the Western Convention for location and development: "The professors must be of much sacred learning, especially in the principles of biblical interpretation, with thorough and comprehensive views of the great doctrine of divine revelation, and also versed in knowledge of human nature and be able by their intellectual grasp and electrifying spirit to develop in the minds of their pupils into active, bold and manly habits, like the free and restless spirits on which they are to set, and yet to give them that holy simplicity as befitting the office and so indispensable to the success of the gospel minister."

Frequent references indicate Howell's sincere continuing support of the theological institute at Covington, a support which he finally withdrew because the president was antislavery. This in the South West is an insuperable objection.

Pastoral Internship

Even before coming to Nashville, Howell had been one of the constituting members of the Virginia Baptist Education Society. He also regarded himself as being one of the original founders of Richmond College.

Both in Virginia and in Nashville, Howell proposed more than once a unique plan for the training of young ministers. It was a kind of internship which he evidently put into operation in the Nashville church. Howell described this plan in an editorial in *The Baptist* (June 7, 1845):

"Two years ago we submitted a plan for Theological Instruction which we still think would be best adapted to our wants. . . . It asks for no outlay for buildings. It proposes no endowments. It asks only for sufficient funds to purchase an ample library. It uses the lecture rooms of churches, and it throws the expense upon the churches. It leaves the support of indigent young men to the churches to which they belong, or others in their vicinity.

"It proposes a course of lectures upon Biblical Criticism and Literature; Ecclesiastical History; Sacred Rhetoric and Pastoral Duties, and Polemic and Systematic Theology, and a Catechism at each successive lecture upon each subject. It requires of those who receive a diploma a collegiate education or an equivalent, and admits ministers and young men, whose age and other circumstances will not allow an extended course of study. . . . The study of Hebrew is prescribed for admission. Lectures to extend through three months and two sessions for graduation. Between sessions students would study other courses of reading, assist pastors, supply destitute neighborhoods."

Richmond he said was a better place to carry out this plan than others, but "Nashville is a suitable place for a Divinity School like this."

Earlier (1836) the Tennessee Baptist Education Society for Ministerial Education had met in conjunction with the Tennessee Baptist Convention. The constitution, offered by R. B. C. Howell and unanimously adopted, committed the organization "to afford licentiates the means of acquiring knowledge to enable them with the greater facility . . . to preach the Gospel of Christ." It called for a subscription of funds to "sustain students in existing schools" at about $150 each. Howell reported that colleges in the state had been requested to "abate" their tuition to such ministerial students, but they had declined. Other states had abated the tuition of ministerial students.

Howell's own Nashville church entered into his plan for ministerial internship. Two young ministers in the church (1840-41) were the brilliant Burleson brothers from Alabama—"Richard B. Burleson, licentate" and "Rufus C. Burleson, licentate." Each was received by letter May 24, 1840, and each was dismissed by letter a few months later. Both later went to Texas where each was associated with Baylor University, Richard as professor and Rufus as president.

Both Burlesons, pursuant to the plan of the pastor, almost certainly lived in homes of the church members, were "sustained" by the church, preached in destitute places under the pastor's direction, while pursuing their studies perhaps at Nashville University.

There were in Nashville in 1845 twenty-six schools of all kinds with 1020 scholars in the winter session and 1200 in summer. The fifteen churches (of all denominations) had 3025 members with 300 in Sabbath schools (about 1000 in the summer).

The Tennessee Baptist Education Society in 1839 resolved "to originate an institution." In consequence, Union University opened its doors for its first session May 2, 1841, at Murfreesborough (sic). Howell maintained a close liaison with Union until his return to Virginia in 1850. When he came back to Nashville in 1857, he was saddened to learn that the school had come under the dominant influence of J. R. Graves and the Landmark movement. A man with Howell's decided temperament could not brook this unhappy and unfortunate development.

"For the Whole South"

Howell contributed to ministerial improvement by his encouragement and perhaps even initiation that led to the establishment in 1859 of the Southern Baptist Theological Seminary. His active influence in that definite direction had its origin in 1847. At the annual meeting that year in Nashville of the American Baptist Indian Missions Howell asked the delegates to remain for consultation on the need for a central Southern Baptist theological seminary.

It was pointed out that there were several small seminaries, such as the one in Covington, but the Southern Convention needed to establish its own distinctive seminary polity. They needed a trained ministry, trained by the Southern Baptist Convention in the Bible, "in all learning necessary to its exposition and to the effectual discharge of the pastoral office." In further elaboration of seminary purpose, the consultants concluded that the central theological institution should impart to its pupils "a complete and perfect knowledge of the word of God, and of all those departments of learning necessary to its correct exposition, and to the effectual discharge of the pastoral office." The seminary should be "for the whole South, in a central location."

"The South West," Howell wrote in 1837, "must have its own Theological School. It should be in Nashville."

Arguing for one theological seminary as opposed to several small ones, it was pointed out that a central institution would "combine the faculties, the endowments, the students, and the libraries of the existing seminaries in the south." This, Howell wrote in his Memorial, was "done in 1859, and the results will be seen in all parts, instantly."

Meantime, the lively question of the establishment of a central seminary came up for discussion by Southern Baptists, at their abbreviated meeting in Nashville in 1849 (when cholera caused adjournment to Charleston), in 1851 again in Nashville when Howell was first elected Convention president, and in the successive meetings in 1853, 1855, and 1857.

Howell was in the president's chair in 1857 when the drive for a central seminary finally came to a vote. The Southern Baptist Convention adjourned to "give place to the Education Convention" to meet and in Louisville (1857) authorized the establishment of the Seminary in Greenville.

However, by this date Howell was under considerable pressure to return from Richmond to the Nashville pastorate. That pressure, both internal and objective, undoubtedly had its origin in the growing turmoil of his beloved Nashville flock, now beset by the vociferous and unceasing assaults of the Landmark triumvirate. That awesome threesome (Graves, A. C. Dayton, J. M. Pendleton) had fastened their tentacles on the Nashville scene until Howell found no rest until he acceded to the urgent plea to return. This he did following the 1857 Convention in Louisville.

When Howell returned, the Landmark embroilment drained Howell of energy and of time. Thus diverted to local problems that would not wait, he had neither the time nor the energy to participate in the evolving development of a central seminary. Otherwise the launching of the seminary would most certainly have claimed the major attention of a man of Howell's spirit and drive and vision.

7

The Road Emerges

The widespread notion that slavery provoked the formation of the Southern Baptist Convention has, of course, strong validity in fact. Slavery indeed was *the* issue of the whole body politic in 1845— in government, in economics, as well as in religion.

Methodists were in the throes of disunion. Presbyterians were suffering the pangs of separation. Baptists, North and South, painfully realized that the days of working together in a common cause were numbered. In each case it was the agitation over slavery that was driving the denominations apart.

Taking note of these upheavals, R. B. C. Howell commented in *The Baptist*: "Division is now the order of the day. God grant that the religious revulsions may not lead to a dissolution of our Federal Union."

Fear of that very political sundering was expressed by the *Baptist Banner* of Kentucky: "Our great political fabric adheres mainly by the integrity with which the three great religious denominations in this country cohere; and if they are once sundered, political combinations will scarcely be sufficient to preserve the Union."

That tragic prospect, the same editor felt, was plainly evident in the mounting conflicts within the denominations. "The Methodists," he said, "seem to be hopelessly divided; the Presbyterians are very much agitated upon the same question." Turning to his own brethren, he begged, "Let not the churches despair of preserving the union. We hope our brethren in the south will pause and seek to God for wisdom before they take a step which cannot be retraced."

The "union" to which he referred was the Triennial Convention.

This was the organization, or "mission society," which Baptists throughout the entire nation had created in 1814 to "elicit, combine and direct" their energies "in one sacred effort for sending the word of life to idolatrous lands."

Luther Rice, true to his word to the Judsons in Burma, upon his return toured the States to gather funds for the support of the missionary couple who had remained in that distant land. Everywhere Rice organized mission societies—in New England, up and down the Seaboard, as far west as Nashville. William T. Brantly the elder, before becoming pastor in Philadelphia, had been corresponding secretary of the Savannah Society for Foreign Missions. It had been an appeal in Tennessee by Luther Rice for foreign missions which provoked the snide remark by Elder Parker that he might be willing to give a counterfeit half dollar to missions but he certainly would not throw in any real money for such an object.

Diligent and persistent, Rice had of course influenced in South Carolina a warmspirited man like William Bullein Johnson whom Hortense Woodson aptly calls (as the title of her biography) *Giant in the Land.* She reports Luther Rice as giving credit to William Bullein Johnson for proposing a meeting to organize "some general concert of action" by all the mission societies that Luther Rice had set up.

Johnson (as reported by Woodson) addressed the mission societies in Georgia and South Carolina proposing that delegates from all the societies convene "in some central situation in the United States for the purpose of organizing an efficient and practicable plan, on which the energies of the whole Baptist denomination, throughout America, may be elicited, combined and directed, in one sacred effort for sending the word of life to idolatrous lands."

The upshot was the formation in Philadelphia of the Triennial Convention in 1814. Richard Furman of Charleston was made the first president and William Bullein Johnson, also a South Carolinian, was president in 1844 at the session the year prior to the organization of the Southern Baptist Convention in 1845. Also in 1844, R. B. C. Howell was a vice-president of the Triennial Convention, held again in this eleventh triennial meeting in Philadelphia.

In the 1844 session Johnson had requested not to be reelected, on the ground that the South had supplied the presiding officer twenty-one years and the middle states nine years of the Convention's thirty-year history. Accordingly, Francis Wayland, president of Brown University in Providence, Rhode Island, was elected president.

To the organizing session in 1814 Johnson had gone alone from Georgia, driving his horse to his "chair." Thirty-three had attended the first session to organize the Triennial Convention, 458 the last session in 1844. Of the original thirty-three, Johnson remarked that only seven were still living in 1844.

Baptists in the Southwest were also involved in the General Convention of Western Baptists, begun in 1834. It was composed of "delegates from Churches, Associations, Mission Societies, Education Societies, Sunday School and Tract Societies in good standing in the Baptist denomination, with such brethren in regular standing in Baptist churches as choose to attend and cooperate with us." The stated business of the Convention was to "promote missions, ministerial education for those licensed by churches, Sunday Schools, Religious periodicals, Tract and Temperance Societies and all others warranted by Christ in the gospel."

Two years after his removal to Nashville, R. B. C. Howell was elected president of the Convention of Western Baptists and took part in the organization of the Western Baptist Education Society. He had also been president of the Tennessee State Convention which had as its object (similar to conventions in other states), "to preach the gospel to the destitute." This object was fulfilled by supporting the ministry in communities where Christian strength was insufficient financially to maintain a preaching ministry.

A Painful Division

When Baptists of the South met in Augusta in 1845, they appointed a committee to prepare an address of the Convention "To the Brethren in the United States . . . and to all candid men." The opening sentence sets the tone of the three printed pages: "A painful division has taken place in the missionary operations of the

American Baptists." The next states the subject: "We would explain the origin, the principles, and the objects of that division, or the peculiar circumstances in which the organization of the Southern Baptist Convention became necessary."

The printed statement was signed by William B. Johnson as Convention president. Johnson later explained that the committee including himself, T. Curtis, Richard Fuller and C. D. Mallary had an understanding as to content when they met in Augusta, but that they vested in T. Curtis the responsibility for the actual writing of it.

The entire document of 2500 words is instructive. It reveals with clarity the understanding of the framers of the Convention of the involvement of slavery—that slavery itself was not the cause, but that the divergence of social practices in the effect on missionary operations made impossible the continuance of their union.

Background to the Address

The sentence immediately above compresses a whole volume which calls for some background fill-in even before one can with reasonable expectation of comprehension attempt an understanding of the address itself.

First, it must be remembered that in the South slavery was no moot question in 1845. It was a fixed, deeply entrenched, unchanged, and unchangeable social institution. As such a firmly established practice, slave-holding was not uncommon among pastors—and even by missionaries.

"If Colonel Hall were to die tomorrow," R. B. C. Howell pointed out, "so would be [slaveholders] Mr. and Mrs. Shuck." The darlings even then of missionary Baptists everywhere—J. Lewis Shuck and his wife, missionaries to China—were themselves so caught up in this normal social custom that Mrs. Shuck herself would become the owner of persons if her father (Colonel Hall) should decease.

It is no wonder that Howell should offer such an exclamation, for he himself was in the same bind. Not that he however thought of it as a bind, but rather as a defacto defense of the institution. Mrs. Howell's mother, Jane Toy, owned slaves and did so until she died in 1859, at which time Mrs. Howell was in the same position as the projected one of Mrs. Shuck.

One of the three unpublished book length manuscripts (hand-written, of course) which Howell left on his death in 1868 was on The Family. In the book are three chapters from a series of ser-mons which Howell preached in his Nashville pulpit. One of them, preached on December 23, 1860, is based on 1 Timothy 6:1-6. It was published in two parts in a Nashvile paper.

Howell said that Christianity does not destroy family relation-ships, that there had always been and always would be three kinds of relationships in the family: parents and children, husband and wife, masters and slaves or servants. Christianity, he said, "sancti-fies that relation, and makes it one of love, of sympathy, and of perpetual benevolence." He concluded that "slavery is legitimate, benevolent, and scriptural."

Morton Howell in his Memoirs confirms his father's sermon. He gives a thumbnail sketch, even to their deaths, of the domestics with whom he and the other seven children had lived in the Howell family. Morton says that "when the Negroes were freed by Lin-coln's proclamation," Aggy remained and would not listen to any-body who talked to her of freedom, "without a word as to freedom or wages or anything of that kind."

Granted, Howell's sermon was preached in December 1860, only a few months before the heat of civil conflict blazed into full-scale war. By that time, the intensity of feelings had been fanned by the long smolderings that would soon burst into hot flames. Really, Howell's views about slavery being "legitimate, benevolent, and scriptural" are mild for the times. What else would you expect of a man who had grown up in that day, and who himself had enjoyed in his own home the convenience of domestic servants?

More typical of the earlier period were letters to the editor of the *Christian Reflector* written in 1844 by Richard Fuller of Beaufort, South Carolina. Fuller had attended the Triennial Convention meeting that year in Philadelphia. He had been vocal on the then explosive subject of slavery, as had many others from North and South. Finally the Convention had unanimously passed a resolution disavowing any position, for or against, slaveholding as a factor in the appointment of missionaries and officers.

Following the long and animated discussion, Fuller was requested by the editor of the *Christian Reflector* to express his views for publication. "I do deny that slavery is a moral evil," the South Carolinian wrote in his first letter. "This is the thing affirmed and denied. You say slavery is itself a sin; it is therefore always a sin; a sin amid any circumstances; a crime which must involve the criminal in perdition unless he repents; and should be abandoned at once, and without reference to consequences. This is the abolition doctrine; and at Philadelphia it was reiterated in every variety of phrase; and when even moderate men, and men seemingly very kind and calm in private, mounted the rostrum and felt the oratorical afflatus, we invariably heard, not arguments, but denunciation of this sort; we were sure to have eternal changes rung on the moral evil of slavery, the sin of slavery, the abominable guilt of slavery, to be told that the ineffable horrors of slavery did not admit of discussion, and to be seriously asked what article of the decalogue slavery does not violate."

Quite evidently the one point Fuller was determined to refute was that slavery was always a sin. This he denied. He pointed out that slavery existed throughout the Bible, both Old and New, and that the inspired writers never once attacked it as sinful.

Fuller's racy pen continued for some five thousand words. Immediately Francis Wayland, president of Brown University and newly elected president of the Triennial Convention, wrote in reply. Ultimately their correspondence, all published in the *Christian Reflector,* stretched to a total of fifteen letters, seven by Fuller and eight by Wayland.

Later (in 1845) the letters were published filling 254 pages of fine print, under the title *Domestic Slavery as a Scriptural Institution.* "Never before, I presume," Francis Wayland wrote in the introduction, "has the defence of slavery on Christian principles been so ably conducted. Never before, I think, has any thing been written so admirably calculated to make a favorable impression on those who hold the opposite opinion. . . . If the disciples of Christ, by more clearly perceiving the sentiments of each other, shall find that the ground for the exercise of Christian charity is both wider and firmer than they had apprehended, some good at least will have arisen from this discussion."

Fuller was plainly angered—and other Southerners with him—by the apparent accusation that slaveholding was always a sin. The next year in Augusta those who formed the Southern Baptist Convention said that they had done so because they had been forbidden to preach the gospel to the heathen. The Acting Board of the Triennial Convention had taken the position that they would not appoint slaveholders as missionaries.

In effect, Baptists in the North were saying that Baptists in the South who held slaves were great sinners, that they, therefore, were not worthy to be missionaries. Those in control in the Triennial Convention could not reconcile themselves to any participation in slavery, implied or explicit. Baptists in the South, thus blocked from engaging in missions, were forced to separate if they were to continue their missionary enterprise.

The intensity of their feelings had sparked the tinder that blazed in 1845 in Augusta.

Two Blows to Foreign Missions

Proof of that intensity is the assessment by Howell of two current happenings, one a strange, almost startling provocation, and the other a readily realized logical development. "Two blows," the editor wrote in March 1845, "have, within a few weeks past, been inflicted upon our Foreign Missions, from which we fear the cause cannot soon recover. One is contained in a letter from brother Mason, a missionary in Burmah; and the other in a late decision of the Acting Board in Boston, in answer to the resolutions of the Alabama Convention at its last session."

The letter from Mason, Howell published in *The Baptist:* "I have an invincible hatred to slavery, and I shall say so," Mason wrote from Burma. "It is the foulest blot on the American flag . . . in all nations. I believe it to be the greatest sin that ever clothed itself under the cover of Christianity, that was ever attempted to be defended from the Scriptures. . . . If it be right to run away from persecution as our Saviour taught, surely it is right to run away from Slavery. . . . I have therefore the pleasure to inclose an order for $10 on our Treasurer . . . to assist in the escape of runaway slaves."

Howell's vitriolic pen in response to this outrage was typical of that of other Southern editors. "We send our money to the missionaries in Burmah," the incensed Howell wrote, "to aid them in prosecuting their missionary work among the heathen. We care not a straw, about their sentiments as to the question of slavery, so long as they preach the Gospel, and attend to their proper business. They have all done their duty, so far as we know, up to this time.

"We regret, exceedingly, that brother Mason, who we believe, is an Englishman, has violated our confidence. We will not visit his sins upon his associates. As to him, we must say, that since we find, instead of using our funds for the purpose intended by the donors, he sends them back to New York and pays them to a society whose nefarious work is—'To aid runaway slaves in escaping from their masters,' we shall, surely, forward him no more. If we send money to him, we, thereby, indirectly contribute the means by which our own slaves are kidnapped and dragged off! Brethren, will you do this? We know you will not."

With one voice Baptist editors in the South lashed out against the lawlessness which they saw to be inherent in Mason's act.

The Alabama resolutions, asking for a direct answer as to the appointment of a slave holder as a missionary, brought into focus the fomenting abolition issue. Beginning with their general organization for missions in 1814 (the Triennial Convention), Baptists North and South had engaged together with warm fellowship in the missionary enterprise.

They had worked side by side, both nonslaveholders and slaveholders, without question about slavery. In summary of the consistent policy, Howell wrote in 1845: "They aver that slaveholders as well as non-slaveholders, are unquestionably entitled to all the privileges and immunities which the constitution of the General

Convention [Triennial] permits and grants to its members" and
that "they, as a Board, do not call in question the social equality
of the slaveholder, as to all the privileges of the Foreign Mission
Union."

This summation of their years of hearty cooperation Howell
penned in response to "The late decision of the Acting Board in
Boston."

That decision came as a consequence of the growing agitation
generally over slavery. Abolitionism had spread in the North with
the fervor of militant evangelism. Poets (like Whittier and Long-
fellow) and politicians (Adams and Webster) and preachers
(Wayland and Beecher) had preached the doctrine of liberation
so fervently that Southerners felt that they had some reason to
term them fanatics.

Uncertain Compromise in 1844

The polarization of North and South on the question of slavery
at last permeated Baptist ranks until it became the principal issue
of open debate in Philadelphia at the 1844 sessions of the Triennial
Convention. At that meeting a delegate from New York called for
"a committee to consider dissolution of the Society or report alterations of the Constitution that will admit of cooperation of those
who have conflicting views on slavery." Richard Fuller of South
Carolina proposed a resolution disclaiming any involvement in
slavery or antislavery.

At length a compromise was reached by which the Convention
went on record as disclaiming "all sanctions, either expressed or
implied, of slavery or anti-slavery."

Although this compromise was reached after full and thorough
understanding in sessions of Baptist leaders from South and North
and its text had been published widely throughout the country,
the Baptists of Alabama were still suspicious when they met in their
annual state convention that fall (1844). Would the Acting Board
in Boston appoint a slaveholder if one applied for missionary appointment?

Earlier a slaveholder had applied. He was refused.

The Alabama resolutions asked for a direct answer. The Acting Board gave it: "If any one should offer himself as a missionary, having slaves, and should insist on retaining them as his property, we could not appoint him. . . . One thing is certain, we could never be a party to any arrangement which implies approbation of slavery."

The response from South and North was as immediate and as direct as was the provocative decision of the Acting Board (which managed missionary operations as an executive board for the Triennial Convention). "It is an outrage on our rights," cried the *Religious Herald* of Virginia.

The Christian Index of Georgia agreed. That paper had issued a half sheet setting forth the facts and reviewing the grounds of the recent refusal of the American Baptist Home Mission Society to employ Rev. James E. Reeves (a slaveholder) as a missionary.

The board of directors of the Alabama Convention, meeting in a special called session in response to the decision of the Acting Board, voted to retain their mission funds until the next meeting of the Triennial Convention (in 1847), named a committee of three to reply to the Boston board, expressed the conviction that it was expedient to hold a convention of the Baptists in the South, and appointed fourteen delegates to such a convention.

There was also a called meeting of the board of managers of the General Association of Kentucky. "We do not advocate slavery," they concluded, "but we abhor the thought of being repelled from the brotherhood merely because we are slaveholders." The late decision was "an unjust violation" not only of thirty years bond but of a social and harmonious decision at the last Triennial Convention.

Many felt that the problem was aggravated by the Acting Board's location in Boston. "We must remove the seat of the Board from the center of fanaticism," insisted the *Baptist Banner* of Kentucky. The hope for Baptists, this editor felt, was to relocate the board in Washington, Baltimore, or Richmond. This, he argued, will "effectually cure the evils under which we now labor."

Howell in *The Baptist* published the resolutions of many Asso-

ciations most of which called for withholding of funds from the
Boston Board and all agreeing with the proposals of a southern
convention to face the issue. Over the span of a few weeks *The
Baptist* published editorial comments from papers in Maine, Pennsylvania, Michigan, Alabama, Kentucky, New York. Typical was
this from the Michigan *Christian Herald*: "We have for a long
time been confident that a separation must ultimately take place
between the northern and southern Baptists. As long as slavery
exists . . . will there be difficulty."

Even a man like Francis Wayland, president of Brown University,
writing to a friend in the South, admitted that "you will divide"
as you should.

A man who signed himself "a plain country preacher" wrote in
the *Banner and Pioneer* that the Board in Boston had decided the
matter of slavery "with all the gravity of a conclave of Bishops,
acting as lawyers to the churches, nor do I wonder that they have
done so. Enough has been said and done by brethren in different
sections to puff the Board into the bladder consequence they now
assume. I have heard good brethren talk with horror about a
western organization, and seen them tremble like aspen leaves at
the thought of offending the Boston Board. They are now reaping
the fruits of their doings. I do not feel disposed to 'weep with
them that weep.' On the contrary, I rejoice rather, for when Baptists, who boast that their churches are sovereign and independent,
so far forget themselves as to look upon a mere missionary Board
as the great bond of union and as indispensable to religious cooperation, I can but hail with pleasure the providence that commends
the cup of such folly to their lips."

The answer, "the plain preacher" believed was not to withdraw—
"No, never!" for this "is indirectly to sanction the deed, and to
encourage officers in similar courses by licensing them to believe
that such practices may be indulged in with impunity, that Boards
of benevolent associations are irresponsible to the authors for their
being!"

The plain preacher was outvoted, although Howell himself seemed
inclined to agree. The Virginia Baptist Foreign Mission Society

issued a call for the meeting in Augusta, and Baptists in all of the
states throughout the Southeast made ready their delegations.

Howell Counseled Delay

Howell felt that the call was made too hastily, that he himself
and others from Tennessee could not at a moment's notice make
the four or five hundred mile trip by horseback, and that the whole
idea of immediate secession was premature. In a letter addressed to
the president of the Augusta convention, he counseled delay until
after the forthcoming Triennial Convention in Cincinnati in 1847
should have an opportunity to confirm or reject (as he thought
they would) the action of the Acting Board.

If they did go forward with the meeting as proposed by the
Virginia Society, Howell suggested that it be held in Nashville.
His associate editor, William Carey Crane, agreeing with his senior
editor, pointed out that it would be much less expensive to reach
Nashville than Augusta. From Alabama, Mississippi, Louisiana and
Tennessee he said it would cost from $60 to $100 one way to
Augusta. In contrast, even from Virginia it would cost only $40
to reach Nashville via Baltimore and Cincinnati. From Georgia and
South Carolina, by railroad and stage, it would be $40. From Ken-
tucky, Mississippi, Alabama, Missouri and Florida to Nashville
Crane said the expense would be only $15 to $30.

The Tennessee Baptist Foreign Mission Society, in special session
responding to the call from Virginia to meet in Augusta, concluded
by official action (reported by *The Baptist*, April 12, 1845) that (1)
the resolutions (of compromise) at the last Triennial Convention
"amounted to instructions to the Acting Board"; (2) regretted that
Alabama was led to suspect that the Board did not intend to obey
these instructions; (3) lamented that the Board upon the Alabama
interrogation had forfeited the confidence of the whole church; (4)
repudiated all idea of dissolution of Foreign Mission Union; (5) presumed that the Convention will not sustain the Board; (6) meantime
would continue to send funds to the Boston Board to be appropri-
ated "as our Board shall direct."

According to the record of their proceedings, the Tennessee

Society voted to transmit to the Boards of the Triennial Convention "soon to convene in Providence, Rhode Island, and to the Convention proposed to be held in the South."

The Separation Explained

So the events throughout the South moved inexorably to the historic gathering set for Augusta on "Thursday before the second Lord's Day in May next." And when they had met and had accomplished the purpose which had brought them together, the trusted committee made up of their three most able men prepared the document "To the Brethren in the United States; to the congregations connected with the respective Churches; and to all candid men."

"A painful division has taken place in the missionary operations of the American Baptists," they admitted thoughtfully. "We would explain the origin, the principles and the objects of that division, or the peculiar circumstances in which the organization of the Southern Baptist Convention became necessary."

In detail the three and a half pages of fine print in the 1845 S. B. C. annual pointed out that the separation followed thirty years of cordial cooperation without respect to slavery or anti-slavery, that it had been marked by a happy, even joyfully warm interplay of comradeship, and that never had any show of doctrinal difference marred their good fellowship.

When the slavery issue began to trouble their strong bonds, the resolute determination to disallow these disputes to interpose any separating wedges had marked their meetings. Even at the last Triennial sessions it had been almost unanimously "Resolved, That in co-operating together, as members of this Convention, in the work of foreign missions, we disclaim all sanction, either expressed or implied, whether of slavery or anti-slavery; but as individuals, we are free to express and to promote, elsewhere, our views on these subjects, in a christian manner and spirit."

Less than six months after the solemn passage of that resolution, the Acting Board had innovated this contradictory decision: "If anyone shall offer himself for a missionary, having slaves, should insist on retaining them as his property, they could not appoint him."

In concluding their explanation "to all candid men," the paper signed by Johnson, and concurred in by R. Fuller, T. Curtis, and C. D. Mallary, summed it up in one short phrase from the Apostle: "FORBIDDING US *to speak* UNTO THE GENTILES." The action of the Boston Board limited, even prevented, their missionary operations. Being shut out from appointment, they were effectively prevented from speaking to the Gentiles. This prohibition they could not endure. Slaveholding Baptists in the South were determined to engage in missions.

"One thing is certain," the report added, "we can never be a party to any arrangement for monopolizing the Gospel; any arrangement which . . . would first drive us from our beloved colored people . . . and then cut us off from the whitening fields of the heathen world—with the low moan, for spiritual aid, of the four millions of half stifled Red Men, our neighbors; with the sons of Ethiopia among us, stretching forth their hands of supplication for the gospel, to God and all his people . . . . Our eyes and our hearts are turned with feelings of parental fondness to Burmah and the Karens; with a zeal in which we are willing to be counselled by God and all considerate men, (but by none else,) to the continent of Africa, and her pernicious fountains of idolatry, oppression and blood, but yet more, with unutterable hope and thankfulness, to China and her providentially opened ports, and teeming thirsty millions. Among us, in the South, we have property, which we will offer to the Lord and his cause, in these channels—some prudence with which we would have our best wisdom to dwell; and professions of a piety which we seek to have increased and purified, like that of the first Baptist churches, when they had 'rest; and walking in the fear of the Lord, and in the comfort of the Holy Ghost, were multiplied.' "

Even in that moment of small beginnings, William B. Johnson and his compatriots looked to the future with prophetic hope: "Above all," they wrote as a final sentence, "the mountain pressure of our obligations to God, even our own God; to Christ and to Him crucified; and to the personal and social blessings of the Holy Spirit and his influences, shall urge our little streams of the water of life to flow forth; until every wilderness and desolate place within our reach (and what extent of the world's wilderness wisely considered is not within our reach?) 'shall be glad—even at this passing calamity of division; and the deserts of unconverted human nature 'rejoice and blossom as the rose.' "

"Ready for the Event"

On the very week set for the Augusta meeting—"Thursday before the second Lord's Day in May next"—South Carolina Baptists met in Edgefield at the call of their president, William Bullein Johnson. The man who thirty years before had proposed a general convention to "elicit, combine and direct" their common energies of the denomination, now presided as his state named the delegates to Augusta. That meeting in Edgefield was on May 3, 4, 5. The one in Augusta was set to begin on May 8.

Of the upcoming sessions Johnson wrote as reported by Hortense Woodson: "A new channel must be created through which the liberality of the Southern and South Western Baptists shall flow. . . . I have been brought to this conclusion by slow and painful steps. It was my privilege . . . to be associated with that noble band . . . who organized the General Missionary Convention . . . . But now . . . there comes an awful irruption upon us, cleaving the body in twain. Its indications were at first small, but they have enlarged and multiplied. What it was in the power of our feeble efforts to do in arrest of their progress, and in prevention of the catastrophe, has been done, but all in vain. I, therefore, bow submissively to the overruling Providence of Him who maketh darkness His pavilion and the thick clouds His chariot, and am ready for the event" (*Giant in the Land*, p. 117).

8

These Made It to Augusta

In retrospect and in view of the slow means both of communication and of travel, it really is amazing that even a corporal's guard was able to get together and do a respectable job of business in Augusta in May, 1845.

Consider first the very short time limit imposed. The call for the Augusta meeting was made by the Board of the Virginia Foreign Mission Society. It was published in the *Religious Herald* of March 13, 1845. It proposed a convention in Augusta on "Thursday before the second Lord's Day in May." That would be on May 8, less than two months away.

In that brief time span Baptists in states, associations, and "societies" would need to respond as to participation and attitude. Appointment of delegates to the meeting would have to be made, the host church in Augusta would have to prepare for uncertain but sure-to-be considerable delegations. Decency of the genteel visitors required some confirmation to the Augusta hosts of the numbers who would come and would be guests in homes.

All of these meticulous preparations were made without benefit of modern means of communication. Indeed 1845 antedated the telephone—and availability of the telegraph, the first line between Baltimore and Washington having been built the previous year. Mail, the principal means of communication, was slow. And the preparations—all of them—for a historic and sizeable gathering had to be completed in less than two months.

The wonder is that anyone got there. Our friend Howell didn't—in part for the very reasons noted above. But he stayed away also for sincere doubt, not at the ultimate need to separate but for reasons of poor timing, which he stated pointedly. He himself would not attend, and he doubted that anyone from Tennessee, Mississippi, Arkansas, Missouri or Kentucky would be present.

"We should not as yet secede," he urged in a letter to the Convention president. His letter was read to the gathering as were others from those unable to attend. (1) It would be giving too much importance to the action of the Boston Board. They are but the agents of the Convention (Triennial). (2) To secede at this juncture would manifest disrespect for the large number who disapprove of the late decision of the Boston Board. (3) It is very probable that the Convention will not sustain the Board. [By this he meant even those in the North who regretted the Boston action.] "I, for one, desire that that body shall have the opportunity of rebuking its unfaithful agent. If it does, there is no reason for secession. If it approve, our imperative duty will be to withdraw and form a Southern organization. Let us go up to the next Triennial Convention, get our demands admitted, and remain in the union."

Howell also pointed out that he could not depart at a moment's notice on a 400 or 500 mile journey by horseback over the mountains. He doubted his state would be represented in Augusta—which it was not.

Even though Howell's letter, along with similar ones from other directions, was read to the respectful assemblage, and Howell was elected a vice-president *in absentia*, some raised questions as to his loyalty to the new Convention. When the editors of the *Religious Herald* in Virginia and of *The Christian Index* in Georgia had a few choice questions about the Tennessean's loyalty, Howell, with characteristic spirit, bluntly suggested that if these two editors didn't mend their speech Tennessee might not be represented next year at the 1846 sessions in Richmond. Feelings evidently were smoothed, for Howell, in succession, was elected vice-president or president as long as he lived (except in 1863 again in Augusta which war time expediences prevented him from attending and in 1867 in Memphis by which time he had already had the stroke which was his fatal illness.)

In view of the focus in these pages upon Howell's contribution to the development of Convention polity, it is appropriate here to point out a series of interesting paradoxes.

First, as already noted, Howell did *not* attend the Augusta meeting. And yet, by his letter and his editorials, he most certainly influenced the deliberations of that body.

Then, even in his absence he was elected a vice-president—clear evidence that he was regarded as a person to be taken into account by the infant body of Baptists.

Even more paradoxical was the later event of his most significant imprint on denominational polity. This most pronounced impress on polity began to emerge when Howell was Convention president, but the strange circumstances were such that precisely for polity reasons he could not perform the required service while in the president's chair. To serve the Convention, he resigned as president in order to implement basic polity. He could serve the Convention at the point of polity only by freeing himself from official Convention relationship.

In a sense then in these three paradoxes he saved his life by losing it. He served by being absent.

Johnson Was Ready

But in 1845 the crowd did come, on short notice, and with minds and hearts ready for what William Bullein Johnson called "the event." No one was readier than Johnson himself. Tall, erudite, almost feeble, but clear to the point as an arrow—Johnson was truly the man of the hour for that strategic moment. There was simply no one else even to be considered for president.

His proposal had led to the organization of the Triennial Convention in 1814. He had stated the classic terms of its purpose, which were carried forward into the Augusta constitution to elicit, combine, and direct the energies of the denomination for the propagation of the gospel. Much else from his pen found apt preservation in Augusta. It is indeed fairly accurate to say that Johnson was largely the father of both constitutions, that of the Triennial in 1814 and of the Southern in 1845.

Moreover, Johnson had as recently as the previous year stepped down from the presidency of the Triennial Convention to give way to Francis Wayland, a northerner. In his maturity and long experience, Johnson, although now nearing the close of his active years, was the choice for president in Augusta. And after he had presided, the newly created Foreign Mission Board made him their agent—a happy choice of a trusted patriarch to succeed to the shoes of Luther Rice as a traveling agent to raise money for the infant Foreign Board.

It was Johnson, as temporary president, who urged the assembled delegates in Augusta to proceed at once to organize. Some doubt had been expressed, even by Johnson himself, as to the powers of the Convention to elect even a provisional government. Ultimately, it was the president's judgment that they did have such power and that such organizing should precede all else. He was of the opinion that the adoption of the Constitution brought the delegates who formed the Convention into its membership and that the election of officers should be the first order of business. Accordingly, officers were elected. Johnson thus kept the chair, with Lumpkin, Taylor, Dockery, and Howell as vice-presidents. Jesse Hartwell of Alabama and J. C. Crane of Virginia were made secretaries.

The Great Question Before the Body

The main issue of the meeting claimed attention on the second day.

"The resolution declaring it expedient to form a separate organization," Editor Sands reported in the *Religious Herald*, "was then taken up. As this was the great question on which was hinged all the future action of the Convention the discussion was entered on with due solemnity, and feeling of the importance of the result. During the debate a fervent prayer was made by Elder Mallary of Georgia. Invitations were given to anyone who had doubts as to the propriety of a separate organization to make them known, but not a dissenting voice was heard. After the resolution had been fully and freely discussed for the space of three hours, the question was taken and the vote was unanimous."

The man who put that historic resolution to the vote in Augusta

(William Bullein Johnson) was a native of South Carolina. His biographer, Hortense Woodson, aptly calls him *Giant in the Land* (her book title). She reports that he had been pastor in Savannah and for twenty-two years in Edgefield where he also directed a female academy. Widely traveled, he had toured the crossroads of Georgia and South Carolina back and forth many times, also as far as New Orleans and into Florida.

The exact language, reminiscent now of terms used again in 1845, that provoked the setting up of the Triennial Convention in 1814, Woodson quotes as follows: Delegates from all the societies Luther Rice had established were invited by Johnson to "convene in some central situation of the United States for the purpose of organizing an efficient and practicable plan, on which the energies of the whole Baptist denomination, throughout America, may be elicited, combined and directed in one sacred effort for sending the word of life to idolatrous lands." He went alone from Georgia in 1814, driving his horse to Philadelphia where thirty-three hearty souls formed the Triennial Convention.

Thirty-one years later he probably boarded a river boat to go by steamer down to Augusta. Now sixty-three years old, the smooth-faced gray patriarch was in the prime of his wise maturity for presiding in the Augusta sessions.

An anonymous pupil of Johnson is quoted by Woodson as describing her old master in the school room as "erect, dignified, lacking somewhat in sympathy and softness but genial and accessible, a terror to evil doers, scathing in rebuke, but whose commendation was something to work for, sweat for, lose sleep and food for."

S. H. Ford wrote in the *Christian Repository* at Richmond: "He presides with more than common dignity. He possesses all the requisites of a good chairman, good discernment, promptness, and decision in taking the sense of the house, with a clear, open, pleasant voice. . . . One of the neatest and most tidy gentlemen I met with. . . . His face is thin and long, and is made to appear longer by wearing his spectacles on the tip end of his nose. The hair thin, frosty, and long behind, disposed to curl; mouth wide, lips thin, frequently compressed . . . precise, regular and methodical in all his affairs. . . . The Doctor is amiable and kind; of manners most courteous. . . . Emphatically a peacemaker, he seeks every opportunity to banish discord and to promote harmony. He witnessed the efforts of Northern fanatics to sunder the ties that bound together the old Triennial Convention, with deepest regret."

A Man Fervent in Prayer

Another man for the times, and of the times, was Charles Dutton Mallary, native of Vermont but since his youth a resident first of South Carolina and now for many years of Georgia. In the midst of debate on the central question of establishing a separate organization, it was he who offered the prayer which drew sincere commendation from every editor.

In 1830, at the age of twenty-nine, Mallary became pastor of the church in Augusta. After four years he moved to Milledgeville, from which church he resigned to become agent for Mercer University. After three years with Mercer, he began a life of evangelistic and pastoral labors for various churches in Middle and Western Georgia, continuing until 1852 when he retired, in feeble health, to his farm near Albany.

Cathcart's *Encyclopedia* reports that "Dr. Mallary was a man of most uncommon piety, and exerted a more wholesome influence than any other man of the denomination in the state. No other stood higher in the esteem of the brethren; nor did any other of his day, in the truest sense, do more for the cause of God and the denomination in the State. Dawson was a more brilliant orator, and Crawford was more learned and scholarly, but neither surpassed him in the highest and best characteristics, as a preacher, He had clear views of divine truth, and a deep experience of its sanctifying power in the heart. His voice was commanding; his elocution distinct and forcible; his imagination splendid; his language chaste, and his address affectionate and persuasive."

The Augusta *Daily Chronicle & Sentinel*, reporting the sessions with much detail, displayed a moving impression of Mallary's prayer, in this account: "Mr. Nichols here rose and moved that prayer be made by the Rev. Mr. Mallary, which was adopted, and

Mr. M. most fervently and eloquently invoked the Supreme Ruler
to so guide their steps as to justify them to the world and redound
to his own glory and the salvation of mankind.

"This was a most imposing and solemn scene, to witness so large
a deliberative body, in which the young, the middle aged, and the
gray-headed patriarchs of the Church, bowed in humble submission
before their Lord and Master, solemnly invoking his counsels to direct
their footsteps in the path of rectitude."

Other editors of Baptist papers commented similarly upon the
prayer of the craggy-browed Georgia preacher, the immediate consequence of which was a firm unanimous vote to organize the Southern Baptist Convention. Mallary was an appointed delegate to the
Convention from the Rocky Creek Church in Georgia.

A Voluble Spokesman

Almost certainly the most loquacious of all those in the Augusta
meeting was Jeremiah Bell Jeter, 43-year-old pastor of the First
Baptist Church in Richmond. His talkativeness was evidently a long-
standing attribute, for at nineteen immediately upon coming up out
of the baptismal water, from the North Fork of the Otter River, he
gave his first public address. The waters—still saturating his clothing—
were from the chill stream on a December Sunday.

But in Augusta he had ample grounds for his frequent comments.
For one, he of course represented *the* church of Virginia. Moreover,
it was the Virginia Foreign Mission Society that had called the Augusta meeting, and in doing so they had deferred to Augusta rather
than setting the sessions in their own city.

It became evident in the discussion in Augusta that "the churches
and brethren were laboring under misapprehensions of the true
position of the [Boston] Board and of the Baptist denomination
in the South," according to Editor Sands of Virginia. Jeter, who had
only a few days previously attended meetings in Providence of the
several Northern (or General) societies, made a valuable contribution
to an understanding of the firm attitude of the Northern brethren.
Requested to summarize his conclusions, he reported that there was
no possibility of a reversal of the action of the Acting Board. J. H.

Campbell of Georgia who had also been in Providence, confirmed Jeter's opinion.

Almost as talkative as Jeter was the irrepressible Richard Fuller. He had been baptized an Episcopalian and trained as a lawyer, which profession he practiced with considerable success in the high culture of his native antebellum Beaufort, South Carolina.

After his conversion, Fuller became pastor in Beaufort, there gaining a deserved reputation as the preacher without a peer at mid-century. Any of his extant printed sermons will repay the reading, his impassioned eloquence on "The Cross" being as moving a piece of poetry in prose as one can find anywhere.

A year after Augusta, Fuller acceded to a call from Baltimore where he spent the rest of his life. It was Fuller who in 1863, when the Convention met again in Augusta, brought a report on the State of the Nation—and before the report was concluded he was excused from the meeting for safety reasons. (In Baltimore in 1863 he lived in a Border state.)

Although primarily a preacher, Fuller also had ideas on procedure—and he voiced them freely, sometimes to the annoyance of impatient conventioners. The obnoxious J. R. Graves commented editorially about a later meeting that Fuller had spoken *seven* times. The implication was that Fuller liked to hear his own voice, but that it was less than melodious to Graves.

Wholly free and uninhibited, Fuller was on his feet often in Augusta. It was he who reported for a committee that it is "expedient to form an organization for the purpose of carrying on missionary operations of those willing to adhere to the old platform of the Triennial Convention." This was a preliminary resolution to the final enabling unanimous vote which called the Southern Baptist Convention into being.

State Representations

Georgia Baptists appointed 173 delegates to the Augusta meeting, 15 of whom were absent. Among those present was Colonel Wilson Lumpkin of Athens, a former governor, made a vice-president of the Convention and, thus, on the committee to obtain a chater of incorporation from the Georgia Assembly. Alabama certified 37 delegates, including one man named by three different bodies, six other duplicates, and 13 who were absentees. From that state were both Basil Manlys (senior, president of the University; and junior, pastor of country churches). At least a half dozen were delegates from Siloam church in Marion (H. Talbird, E. Baptist, D. P. Bestor, J. H. DeVotie, W. Hornbuckle, T. F. Curtis).

That man T. F. Curtis was an enigma, teacher of theology at the Howard. His father, T. Curtis, on the committee with Johnson, Fuller and Mallary to draw up the address "To all Candid men," had arrived not long since from England and was pastor of Wentworth Church in Charleston. After establishing an academy for girls at Limestone Spring (later Limestone College), he met a premature death in 1858 on a steamer that burned in the Potomac.

But the son was more than a thorn in the flesh to his fellow Baptists, South and North. They made him corresponding secretary of the Domestic Board in the early fifties. Then reelected him to another term. But he declined to serve. Finally he "apostasized" and went to the seminary in Lancaster, Pennsylvania. But there he was always a tempest in the teapot, never satisfied with the salary offered and using every means at hand to get preferential remuneration. His apostasy? You have to read it between the lines, as suggested by the title of a book explaining his philosophy of interpretation: *The Human Element in Divine Revelation.*

If this seems to take us afield from Augusta, bear in mind that it is deliberate to set us right down in the human scene of that dusty Georgia town. There was no pavement in Augusta in 1845.

The Georgia Railroad brought some delegates along the way from as far as West Point. The entire Virginia delegation (39, with 7 absent) came by the cars down to Wilmington. Two from Baltimore joined them in Petersburg. From Wilmington to Charleston passage was by overnight ship.

Sands reports that the passage by steamboat from Wilmington to Charleston "was not very pleasant. During the night we encountered a severe storm, most of the passengers were seasick, and all were glad to reach Charleston."

At Charleston Sands reports that "such a large body of delegates had collected from the lower part of the state, so that we had to wait until an extra car was attached to the train." At various points on the road, delegates joined and the cars became uncomfortably crowded. At Akin another car was added so that on reaching Hamburg, opposite Augusta, Sands said that "we presented the appearance of a little army."

After a full day in the cars from Charleston, they reached Augusta on Wednesday evening about 7 o'clock—at least two days and one night en route from Richmond. Several of the Virginia delegates "proceeded to the hospitable mansion of Dr. W. H. Turpin, the well known and liberal friend of benevolent efforts. The Baptist meeting house is a commodious brick edifice. The church is under the pastoral care of Elder William T. Brantly, the son of the late esteemed and able divine, Dr. William T. Brantly, Sr., for whom the pulpit is still shrouded in black."

The elder Brantly had been pastor in Beaufort, in Augusta, in Philadelphia, and in Charleston. He had died the previous March.

Lodgings and Transportation

The younger Brantly had come to the Augusta pastorate in 1840. As host pastor, he had been busily preparing for the incoming delegates. This notice had been published in *The Index*: "The delegates to the Southern Baptist Convention are requested to report themselves on arrival, to a committee who will be in attendance at the Lecture Room of the Baptist Church to designate the lodgings which have been provided for them. W. T. Brantly, pastor."

There was also this Notice to Delegates: Delegates to the Convention in Augusta will be allowed to pass free by the Railroad and Steamboat line between Petersburg and Charleston, and will be allowed to return free by the Charleston Railroad. Delegates by the Georgia Railroad will only be charged half price going and returning, which will amount to the same thing. Evidence of appointment must of course be produced."

To complete the register of delegates: Maryland, 2; D. C. , 2 (1 absent); North Carolina, 3 (1 absent). South Carolina, 120

(13 absent). Georgia 173 (15 absent). Louisiana, 2. Kentucky, 1 (the venerable Isaac McCoy). Total listed delegates, 379 (50 absent, at least 20 duplicate appointments). Actual number persons present—approximately 309. The secretaries entered in the minutes a disclaimer as to the exact number, saying that there was so much confusion in registration that an exact listing was impossible.

One thing is certain: there was not one woman on the list.

And the most curious entry was that of A. Dockery of North Carolina. A footnote in the 1846 minutes offers the secretary's correction of the spelling of this man's name who was elected a vice-president. He was also named as one of the incorporators of the Convention by the Georgia Assembly. But still the footnote stands as a singular claim to a place in history: Uncertainty as to whether his name was Dockery or Docrey, an uncertainty that has been preserved in succeeding Convention annuals now for more than a century—of a duly appointed delegate who did *not* attend the meeting!

They met day by day in the historic little church on Green Street, their horses tethered to the hitching posts, feet trampling the dry or muddy soil. Inside the building momentous issues were faced in solemnity.

Men of High Eminence

Editor Sands commented that it was "one of the largest assemblages ever convened for religious purposes in the Union. It combined a large portion of the wisdom, talent, and experience of the Southern churches. Ministers who had borne the burthen and heat of the day, others in the vigor of life, several of the young, full of ardor and enthusiasm—of lay members, some who had held, and others now holding high stations in their respective states, ex-governors, generals, judges, lawyers, doctors, etc., and character of high eminence, were to be seen at this Convention.

"All important questions were decided unanimously. On the expediency of separation all were agreed. Not one voice was raised against the decision. All deemed it necessary, politic, and just. On minors there were occasional differences, and at times some little impatience—but for a general concurrence in sentiment, for kindness and forbearance towards each other, we presume this Convention was never excelled by any other body, equally numerous.

"Kindly feelings were invariably expressed for our Northern brethren. It was admitted that we had been treated with injustice, that our rights had been infringed, but no harsh invective was heard, no angry expression uttered. We have begun well, and we trust that our churches will now act, and that henceforth the only strife betwist North and South will be which shall do most to promote the interests of the Redeemer's kingdom and the salvation of their fellow men."

On all counts it was a notable assembly, as attested by the press both secular and religious. Their behaviour was with confidence and calmness. The record they have left shows them to be fully competent to the singular trust that was theirs at their stressful moment in time. The authority on which they acted and the meaning of their decisions claim attention in the immediately succeeding pages.

9

What They Did While There

The assembly in Augusta, May 8-12, 1845, was quite explicit in the enabling actions they took. They spelled it out very clearly: "It shall be the design of this Convention to promote Foreign and Domestic Missions and other important objects connected with the Redeemer's Kingdom, and to combine for this purpose such portions of the Baptist denomination in the United States as may desire a general organization for Christian benevolence, that shall fully respect the independence and equal rights of the Churches."

To add clarity to plain language of purpose, they adopted this familiar preamble: "We the delegates from the Missionary Societies, churches, and other religious bodies of the Baptist denomination in various parts of the United States met in convention in Augusta, Georgia for the purpose of carrying into effect the benevolent intentions of our constituents, by organizing a plan for eliciting, combining and directing the energies of the whole denomination in one effort for the propagation of the Gospel."

Then it was stated that there would be held "a triennial convention [which] shall consist of members who contribute funds, or are delegated by religious bodies contributing funds."

It was also resolved "in accordance with the Second Article" (quoted above in the first paragraph) of the Constitution that "this convention will cordially embrace and affiliate auxiliary societies upon its principles, and recommend to the brethren the formation of such societies."

At least three questions now claim attention: How did the fundamental actions of 1845 parallel the 1814 Convention? In what essentials did the Southern Convention differ from the Triennial? On what authority did the delegates act in 1845?

The third question claims attention first, for it addresses the basic inquiry of polity. Polity is the prime theme of this entire book—polity, or church government, as developed in those strategic years and around the career of that strategic person, R. B. C. Howell. It is no exaggeration to say that everything in his ministry since Howell's steps first touched the Great Valley in July, 1834, had to do with polity.

His first challenge was to rebuild a congregation that had been wooed and won to the "peculiar views of Alexander Campbell"— clearly on the issue of polity or church government. Again it was a debate on church government in 1838 that led to another near-dismemberment of his church. Twenty years later every contention with the Concord Association, or with other associations, centered on government; or the resistance to the deplored trend toward making associations ecclesiastical courts. Suspicions and restiveness about state conventions also brought polity into sharp focus. And the next three chapters, which detail the Howell-Graves imbroglio, center on a conflict which each contestant admitted was a test of polity.

Howell wasn't in Augusta, but a problem which dogged his footsteps for a lifetime was very much there.

Were They "Instructed"?

Were the men in Augusta "delegates" from their churches and societies? They called themselves such. But what did the designation really mean? Were they "instructed" delegates? Certainly in anticipation of the Augusta convention there had been many meetings of Baptist bodies all over the South. These meetings, of state boards, of associations, of churches, of societies, were set specifically in response to Virginia's call for the Augusta convention. These bodies did come to some rather definite conclusions in the light of the known circumstances. Delegates were appointed to express these conclusions in Augusta.

They also called themselves "members" of the Convention, and

they participated cordially within the framework of mutual understanding and commitment. Reading the history now at this date,
and noting the spirit of their actions, did they act essentially as
"messengers" in the same spirit as of today in Southern Baptist life?
Or were they truly a different breed? Were they "instructed" in
every detail, or did they act freely as "members"—or as we would
say today, "messengers?"

Because the implications of these questions is relevant today, the
discussion here will deliberately be taken somewhat out of historical
context. The man to whom Southern Baptists are greatly in debt
for clearing the air as to "messengers" or "delegates" was the
always vocal and often irritatingly persistent T. T. Eaton. It was
his sharp tongue that pointed out in 1907, the Convention meeting
that year for the fifth time in Richmond, that participants were
not "delegates" but "messengers." As a very oral man, he probably
made a speech on the subject, for the idea came through so clearly
that every Southern Baptist even now still knows the distinction.
Eaton moved and it was carried that the word "delegates" in the
preamble of the Convention's constitution (see the second paragraph
of this chapter) be changed to "messengers." The reason (per Eaton):
"so as to state the historical facts, and to correct verbal error." Even
in 1845 those who organized the Convention in Augusta, in Article
III of their adopted constitution, called themselves "members."

Now for nearly forty years I have worked in offices where I have
had ready access to the treasured records of Southern Baptists from
their beginnings. For one extended period it was my happy duty
to dig into these records in the preparation of a historical monograph
on one of the Convention agencies (published under the title,
Epochs of Home Missions).

With avid interest I have pored over these mellowed pages. The
account of President William Bullein Johnson addressing the Convention at its closing session in Richmond on June 15, 1846, "in a
feeling and appropriate manner" lives in my memory like a personal
experience.

Sometimes I feel as if I were standing in that 1846 meeting by the
side of James Huckins as he pleads for the destitute in Texas and

weeping with the president and the other 162 "members" as
J. W. D. Creath stands to state his purpose to resign his four
churches in Virginia in order to go to that land of destitution, my
native state. A lump is in my throat as President Johnson declares
that he and his wife are willing for their sons to go also on such "a
distant errand." One younger Johnson did go to China as a missionary.

I have read the record of those early years, line after line, word
upon word, and also with some diligence through all of the Convention's history. It is most difficult for me to accept the implication
in the word "delegates" that they were not free to vote their own
minds, that they were instructed.

The difficulty is twofold. First, what was the extent or nature
of that instruction? On what issues had they been given specific
directions for casting their ballots?

Had they been instructed on the paramount issue of whether to
set up a new and independent Baptist body? Perhaps so, but yet
we find them plainly saying that they had changed their opinions
and would vote differently from their original intentions. Did each
carry directions on whether to vote for a society form of organization for a convention? On how many societies or boards? On the
content and manner of preparation of the preamble? Of "an address to the public," setting forth the reasons which led to the formation of the Southern Baptist Convention? Were they instructed
on how to vote for the Convention officers? On location of the
boards? On where the next meeting should be held? On the
preacher for the next session?

You see, when you seek to apply the principle of an instructed
delegation in the actual dynamics of a Convention session, the
theory breaks down under the weight of its own absurdities. It is
simply inconceivable that the churches and societies sending delegates to the Convention in Augusta could have anticipated all of
the issues which would be confronted or that the larger constituency
would have felt competent in advance to provide the instructions.
Nowhere do I find in the records any allusion to indicate that the
voting rested on any such instructions.

The second difficulty grows out of a realization of the stature of those men who were "members" of that first Convention. They came, most of them, from wayside places—from County Line and Powelton and Shoulder Bone churches in Georgia, from Mount Gilead and Cuhihatchie (also Siloam and Tuscaloosa) in Alabama, from Mattaponi Church and Shiloh Association in Virginia, from Sandy River and Beach Branch in South Carolina. Richmond and Baltimore, but not Raleigh nor Atlanta nor Knoxville, were represented. But though these men, in the main, were from small places, they certainly towered tall in their behavior.

There was the man selected as president, Rev. William B. Johnson, D.D., theological professor. There was the vocal J. B. Jeter of Richmond who had attended the "late meeting in Providence, R. I." of the General Board of the Baptist General (Triennial) Convention, the curt and summary actions of which Acting Board in Boston had provoked the meeting in Augusta and ultimately the organization of the Southern Convention.

There was Honorable Wilson Lumpkin, former governor of Georgia, a man equal to the assignment of standing before his state legislature to secure the charter for the new Convention. There was the brilliant Richard Fuller of Beaufort, South Carolina—no backwoods town. There was the Englishman from Charleston, T. Curtis, and there was his son, T. F. Curtis, who later, it was said, apostastized. And when one searches for the reason, he gains the suspicion that it was because of the younger Curtis' individualistic emphasis upon the human element in inspiration! There were the two Manlys, the president of the University of Alabama and his brilliant young son, still pastor of rural churches. And there was the rugged Isaac McCoy of Kentucky, whose name even then was a legend wherever men knew about missions among the American Indians.

No, these do not impress you as the kind of men who would submit to the fettering or whose constituency would impose the fettering to the point of not being "free to vote their own minds." They were of a higher caliber, of a taller stature, equal to the independent responsibilities they assumed in the historic assemblage in Augusta.

Although not among them in Atlanta, R. B. C. Howell was certainly one with them in stature and in independence to act responsibly.

Leaders in Freedom

What then was the spirit of their deliberations? The freedom in their actions? The nature of their relation to the constituents?

In their preamble and constitution they said that they were "delegates from Missionary Societies, Churches, and other religious bodies of the Baptist Denomination in various parts of the United States"—but that they were "*members*" of the Convention. They declared the purpose of their meeting to be to carry "into effect the benevolent intentions of our constituents, by organizing a plan for eliciting, combining and directing the energies of the whole denomination in one sacred effort, for the propagation of the Gospel."

As one reads the record of their actions, he does not feel that men are acting under the controlling restraint or instructions of constituents, except only as there is common agreement on the holy purpose stated above. Indeed, they were the leaders, the initiators in organizing that plan "for eliciting, combining and directing the energies of the whole denomination in one sacred effort, for the propagation of the Gospel."

In Article II of their constitution, they stated that it would be the design of the Convention "to promote Foreign and Domestic Missions" and "to combine for this purpose, such portions of the Baptist denomination in the United States, as may desire a general organization for Christian benevolence, which shall fully respect the independence and equal rights of the Churches." No, they were not instructed delegates, but rather they were men with vision and courage and leadership to organize a missionary program and enlist those who were like-minded to join them in its execution.

These were not men with proxies in their pockets, or instructions on how to vote on any given issue, they were prophets of stature and vision and courage and capacity for leadership. With their constituency there was a congeniality of purpose, a mutuality of confidence, members of the Convention and their constituency alike being instructed from within, by the Spirit which motivated them together in this "one sacred effort."

This continues to be the nature of the relationship between those who attend our annual sessions (whether "members," or "delegates," or "messengers") and the larger constituency whom they represent Still there is a congeniality of purpose, an instruction of the Spirit. There must be. Those who have the sharpest motivation, the contagious capacity for leadership, the commitment of heart, attend the annual sessions, not in any sense to decide arbitrarily on programs and budgets, but rather in continuing fulfilment of the purpose to carry "into effect the benevolent intentions of our constituents, by organizing a plan for eliciting, combining and directing the energies of the whole denomination in one sacred effort for the propagation of the Gospel." That purpose expresses the real nature as well as the source and limit of the appropriate instructions properly granted and assumed by those who are competent "members" of any annual session of the Southern Baptist Convention, be it in 1845 or in 1975.

The Striking Parallel

The similarity in content and in style of writing of the constitutions of the Triennial and of the Southern conventions are immediately apparent. Indeed Editor Sands of the *Religious Herald* in his 1845 report admits that "the old constitution of the Triennial Convention served chiefly as the basis of the new one."

Note for instance how closely the Preambles of the two parallel each other:

> *Triennial* (1814): We, the delegates from Missionary Societies and other religious bodies of the Baptist Denomination in various parts of the United States met in Convention in the city of Philadelphia for the purpose of carrying into effect the benevolent intentions of our constituents by organizing a plan for eliciting, combining and directing the energies of the whole denomination in one sacred effort for sending the glad tidings of Salvation to the Heathen and to nations destitute of pure Gospel-light, do agree to the following rules or fundamental principles.

> *Southern* (1845): We, the delegates from Missionary Societies, Churches and other religious bodies of the Baptist denomination in various parts of the United States, met in convention in the city of Augusta, Georgia, for the purpose of carrying into effect the benevolent intentions of our constituents by organizing a plan for eliciting, combining and directing the energies of the whole denomination in one sacred effort, for the propagation of the Gospel, agree to the following rules or fundamental principles.

Then follow, for the Triennial Convention, fourteen articles and for the Southern, thirteen, very similar throughout. Each takes up in order: name, stated meetings, basis of membership or representation in the body, the officers and how they are elected, administration of the work, qualifications of missionaries, duties of executive officers, duties of treasurers, special called meetings, how alterations may be made.

Article II of the 1814 document provided "That a Triennial Convention shall hereafter be held consisting of delegates, not exceeding two in number from each of the several Missionary Societies and other religious bodies of the Baptist Denomination, now existing, or which may hereafter be formed in the United States, and which shall each, regularly contribute to the general Missionary Fund, a sum, amounting at least to one hundred dollars per annum."

In comparison, Article III of the Southern Constitution also provides for a triennial convention consisting of "members who contribute funds, or delegates of religious bodies who contribute," one delegate for each $100 annual contribution or $300 contributed at one time within the three years, two delegates for $200 contributed annually, three delegates for $300, and so on. "Great collateral Societies" were entitled to one delegate for each $1000 contributed annually.

As one further example of similarity, Article I of the Triennial Constitution states: "That this body shall be styled 'The General Missionary Convention of the Baptist Denomination in the United States of America for Foreign Missions.'" Article I of the Southern (1845) document simply says: "This body shall be styled the

Southern Baptist Convention."

The similarities throughout confirm convincingly the Virginia editor's report that the first was the basis of the second. Indeed, sameness of language affords ample internal grounds for suspecting common authorship. One wonders if William B. Johnson may have been the person who strongly influenced that sameness of style and language. He was one of a number, although not the chairman, appointed to draft the 1814 document.

In her biography of Johnson, Hortense Woodson implies, if she does not plainly assert, that the South Carolinian was responsible for the same phraseology in the two constitutions. Almost certainly he worked in advance on the needed fundamental statement for the contemplated new organization. It is indeed very possible that he carried in hand to Augusta his own personal version of the new constitution. That work in advance may be the real meaning of Johnson's written word, also reported by Woodson, that he was "ready for the event."

How They Were Different

The one essential difference in the two constitutions rested on the fact that the Triennial Convention was organized for Foreign Missions only, whereas the Southern Convention had as its stated purpose "Foreign and Domestic Missions and other important objects connected with the Redeemer's kingdom." Thus, the first was in fact a missionary society and the second was designed to embrace all kingdom causes.

It has often been said that the first expressed the "society" form of organization, while the second introduced the "convention" form. This summation is only partially correct, for even the Triennial Convention was termed a "General Missionary Convention," and there are indications that the intent was to give that Convention some responsibilities more inclusive than Foreign Missions only. However, historical accuracy enforces the reminder that the Northern Baptist *Convention* was not organized until as late as 1907 in Washington, D. C., and that "Societies" (for Foreign Missions, Home Missions, Publications) still prevail in the North.

In accordance with the prevailing "society" norm, the Triennial Convention in their Article III set up the "Baptist Board of Foreign Missions for the United States." Their twenty-one Commissioners were given "power for the furtherance of the general objects of the Institution"—that is, to administer the Foreign Missions of the Triennial Convention. It was in fulfilment of that responsibility, and under the shorter designation of the "Acting Board" of Boston (as the twenty-one Commissioners were called), that the now famous reply was made to the Alabama inquiry about the appointment of slaveholders.

In contrast, the Southern Convention in Augusta, true to the "Convention" format, named two Boards, one for Foreign Missions in Richmond and one for Domestic Missions in Marion, Alabama.

Even as early as 1845, Southern Baptists also considered the possible need for other boards. Editor Sands reported that the decision would be reached the following year in Richmond as to the need for a board of publications. In its early history and over a period of several years the Southern Convention had a Bible Board. Also, even before 1850, there was recurring discussion of the need for a central Convention seminary, which became a reality in 1859.

On the last day of the 1845 Convention in Augusta, Monday, May 12, resolutions were adopted, as reported by the *Religious Herald:* 1) Cordially embracing auxiliary societies and recommending the formation of such societies; 2) requesting the several State Conventions to remit funds to the Convention treasurers; 3) that the Aborigines have strong claims on their interest and recommending the churches to sustain the Indian Missionary Association; 4) that the Domestic Mission Board take all prudent measures for the religious instruction of the colored population; 5) that the Foreign Mission Board adjust claims with the Acting Board of the Triennial Convention; 6) agree with the Acting Board to take portions of its missions; 7) apply to the State of Georgia for a charter; 8) that the Domestic Mission Board direct effective attention to aid the present effort to establish the Baptist cause in New Orleans; 9) that we give gratitude to the Great Leader of the Church and recognize the Christian spirit which has governed the deliberations as proof of the divine presence in the origin and prosecution of this organization.

At the Monday afternoon session of the closing day, the Foreign Mission Board announced the appointment of William Bullein Johnson as an agent for twelve months.

Howell Late in Life

Interlude Before the Storm

There is now in the chronology of this account a lapse of a dozen years, 1845-1857. This is due to no cessation in the relation of our central character to the official unfolding of the newly organized convention. On the contrary, it was exactly within these years that R. B. C. Howell served as president of the Southern Baptist Convention.

Howell was first elected to preside in 1851 when the Convention met in Nashville. He was reelected and presided successively at Baltimore in 1853, Montgomery in 1855, and Louisville in 1857. At Richmond in 1859 Howell was elected for a fifth time but he declined to serve. No, Howell was not inactive in Convention affairs or in denominational developments in those dozen years.

But it was relatively a quiet interlude, a quiet before the most turbulent storm in the entire career of this dominant man. It was as if in a relaxed decade he was providentially rested for the great battle of his life.

Earlier it was pointed out that Howell knew three things for certain when he began his ministry in Nashville in 1835. He knew that the Great Valley of the Southwest was *the* area for Kingdom conquest. He knew that Nashville was the keystone in the structural arch. He knew that his personal destiny was on this strategic frontier. These three things he knew. Of a fourth he was convinced, that the effective strategy was the good use of publishing.

One thing, perhaps fortunately, Howell did not know when he came boldly to the Southwest. He did not know that his role would be to restore the wreckage following the devastation of one storm after another. Had he known the extreme waste these storms would leave in their wake, had he foreseen the extremities the ensuing conflicts would exact of his own spirit, would he have come? No one knows. Such speculation is beside the point.

He did come. He became the man for the hour. And in an interlude of relaxation, he gained the needed recruitment for the supreme test which was shortly to come.

In personal retrospect, Howell recorded in his Memorial: "For the third time in forty years the desolation of Baptist churches in Tennessee was complete." The first grew out of the "controversy on Predestination." The second came from the "Reformation under Alexander Campbell." Each of these was doing its worst when Howell arrived in 1835. Third, said Howell, the churches had been "severed and prostrated by the Missionary controversy"—or missions and antimissions.

"Will the Baptists of Tennessee ever be united and labor together continuously in the cause of Christ?" the distraught Howell had entreated. "Scarcely did they recover from one division when they fell into another. Would to God this had been the last! But alas yet another awaited us, still more destructive!"

Meantime, though, the blessed interlude. Perhaps from the present perspective it is no exaggeration to say that the man had to have it. He had labored until the human spirit must have rest. And the dozen years were in advance of as trying an encounter as ever taxed the utmost of any man's energies.

After thirteen years, Howell was relieved gradually of one of his double duties, that of editing *The Baptist.* Then surprisingly, perhaps even to himself, and over the strong objections of his congregation, he resigned the Nashville pastorate to accept a call from Richmond.

Back to Virginia Culture

The attractiveness of that call cannot be overstated. It offered release from the turbulence and the crudeness of the frontier to the refinement of Virginia. And not just to Virginia, but to Richmond—the very epitome of culture, of charm, of settled elegance.

The very ultimate for any pastor was a call from a church in Richmond.

And Howell had earned the respite. He had battled to establish the Baptist cause with a reluctant people until every bone and sinew of his being was weary. He needed the amenities offered by a refined Richmond congregation.

But although Howell left the Southwest and enjoyed the choice fruits of Virginia, his fitful slumber was often shadowed by the continuing Nashville scene. Even before Howell left, the Nashville church had called the fervent Richard Fuller, who promptly declined. Even after securing another pastor, the Nashvile church evidently still did not give Howell up entirely. He was advised of their continuing difficulties. Each time the church lost a pastor, Howell was entreated to return.

The church and the Baptist cause declined sadly in every way, as Howell was made painfully aware. This time it was the enervating influence of so-called Landmarkism that played havoc with the Baptist witness.

The shadow of that malignancy, at first much smaller than a man's hand, had first appeared in this notice which Howell published in *The Baptist,* June 28, 1845 (the very next month after the Augusta convention): "The Rev. J. R. Graves of Lexington, Ky., has arrived in Nashville and wished to conduct a Classical School the next Session. He may be found at the City Hall."

After a while Howell invited the young Yankee from Vermont to become assistant editor of *The Baptist.* Howell certainly lived to rue that day! Enough here simply to say that Graves gradually intruded his imaginative influence on the paper and that Howell seemingly was glad for relief. By the time Howell departed Nashville in 1850 in response to the Richmond call, Graves was in full editorship.

In the time of Howell's residence in Richmond, 1850-57, the influence of Graves and of Landmarkism which he made his platform became *the* issue. This was true not only in Nashville, but it was rapidly becoming the issue throughout the Southern Baptist Convention.

The Nashville church, again pastorless in 1857, begged Howell once more to consider returning to their leadership. Since the Southern Baptist Convention was meeting in Louisville that year, Howell agreed to come by Nashville in May after the Convention adjourned. Thus he met with the pulpit committee and acceded to the importunities of the church.

Inevitably and inexorably, Howell's return to Nashville set him on a course which pointed straight as an arrow to controversy. These two giants, Howell and Graves, would surely clash. It was as clear as the noonday sun. And when they did meet, the dust of their engagement would not settle to this very day. It was admittedly a clash of two strong personalities, but at stake was the nature of the denomination and of Convention polity. It was, beyond question, a controversy of the greatest magnitude. The effect on the Southern Baptist Convention may never subside. Howell's most significant service to the Baptist cause—Graves' too—is centered in this traumatic encounter.

10

The Size of Their Scrap

How do you measure the size of a conflict?
You look at the stature of the belligerents.
You sense the intent of the opponents.
You count the opposing forces.
You weigh the significance of the issues.
You record the immediate consequences.
You assess the aftereffects.
You compare with other like engagements.

Finally, you put all of these assessments together and arrive at a personal judgment as to the actual dimensions of the entire imbroglio.

Admittedly, already to this point words have been used with mean, or even derogatory, connotations. Take the word scrap— used here deliberately. It suggests a picayunish encounter between little men continually harrassing one another with their peccadilloes. Or bickering boys pecking each other harmlessly.

Or the word imbroglio. Even without consulting Webster for the exact definition of an unfamiliar word, one at times is filled with shame before the spectacle of two men occupying themselves and a wide constituency seemingly in much ado about nothing.

Manifestly there is more in the Howell-Graves controversy than appears on the surface. Much more. Three chapters here are no more than a brief summary.

Stature of the Belligerents

First, it was a contest between two giants. Neither Howell nor
Graves was a pigmy. That fact stands as a relevant reality, even
though each in the strange alchemy of human enigma is a personal
paradox.

When the two came to slug it out, toe to toe, as was inevitable
by their natures and in the converging circumstances that they
would, it was no little David and giant Goliath encounter. It was
two big-little men battling to the end.

Look at J. R. Graves, younger of the two. Born in Vermont in
1820, he was now 38 years old when the conflict with 57-year
old Howell erupted in the summer of 1858.

From his youth Graves had a remarkable power with words
and ideas. Often in his career he was noted for speaking two and
three hours to spellbound audiences. Once when the Southern
Baptist Convention was meeting in Waco, in 1883, the report
spread among the delegates that J. R. Graves would be preaching
in a few minutes to a Convention overflow assembly at the Methodist church. The halls and corridors and streets were emptied
as the crowd converged immediately on the Methodist meeting
house to hear the long-whiskered and long-winded Graves.

Yet there was much truth in the appraisal of the Methodist
preacher-politician, William Ganaway Brownlow. Incensed by
Graves' book, *The Great Iron Wheel,* in which Graves called
Methodism "a great iron wheel of episcopacy—moving in absolute
control," Brownlow, with little restraint, made reply in a book he
called *The Great Iron Wheel Examined.*

Brownlow wrote that Graves' paper was "a low, dirty, scur-
rilous sheet." Turning to the editor he penned these choice
words: "Take J. R. Graves in his length and breadth, in his
height and depth, in his convexity and concavity, in his manners
and his propensities, and he is a very little man. . . . For
several years past, in portions of several States, with an unearthly
din, this man has been barking, neighing, bleating, braying, mewing,
puffing, swaggering, strutting."

This reputation for being obnoxious even when right Graves

gained early—Brownlow's classic comment was published in 1853 when Graves was only 33. He was a big man who could act in a small way—the kind of person who is so maddeningly right.

Howell, too, was a complex person, very dominant, very proud, very human.

Put two such opinionated, self-assured men as these to the mat in combat and it is no wonder that the dust will not be settled over a century later.

The Fire in Their Eyes

Certainly, men like these will go at it with consuming intensity. Graves said, "Howell is determined to destroy me!"

Howell said, "By malicious slander and libel, he is bent on destroying the character of a score of leading Southern Baptist pastors and editors."

Graves insisted, "He came back to Nashville for the express purpose of destroying me."

Howell implied, "For personal gain he has attempted to gain control of denominational publishing."

Graves asserted, "He had an understanding with the church committee that he would return to Nashville to destroy me."

Howell charged, "He has worked assiduously to estrange leading members of the church and the pastor."

Graves said that Howell was miffed because Graves in his published *Directory* had omitted the D.D. after Howell's name.

Graves was sure that Howell had drawn up with the church committee the specifications to destroy Graves and that he brought the blue prints in his pocket for this when he returned to the Nashville pastorate in 1857. Graves asserted: "He had frankly avowed his purpose months before to crush me by the disgrace of a church expulsion."

Howell charged Graves with undermining the character and the influence of the pastor with the church.

Graves said: "I knew that my prosecutor had determined and prepared the verdict that should be rendered independent of my innocence or guilt."

Howell named nine "specifications" of deliberate and malicious falsehoods against leading brethren.

Ere long you realize that if you believe a tenth of what either said about the other, you would be forced to the conclusion that the other had horns and carried a fork.

One thing is certain: each contestant went at it with hammer and tongs. It was no child's play to either. The intensity of the combatants lends credence to the immensity of the conflict. At the least, neither of them thought that they were occupied with a matter of small moment. That intensity was at white heat for each.

After the conflict was over, Howell wrote in his Memorial: "If all the afflictions of my life were put together they would not amount to a tenth part of the sufferings which this trial and the events connected with it have cost me."

The burning intensity of each contestant marks some measure of the size of their scrap.

Forces Near and Far

The number of forces engaged also gives some indication of the true dimensions. It was indeed a local controversy, and it was on the basis of its local nature, when the obstinate problem thrust itself on the denominational scene, that the Southern Baptist Convention, by accepting Howell's resignation as president, withdrew itself from further involvement. But that very involvement betrays the certainty of a scope far beyond the local.

The local aspect was dire enough. The matter came to a head in the trial of J. R. Graves by the First Baptist Church of Nashville. Four charges against Graves of "grossly immoral and unchristian conduct" were brought by two members of the church. This was at a regular business meeting of the church on September 8, 1858. Later two other members brought a fifth charge of malicious and deliberate falsehood.

It then required three additional church meetings—one of them lasting until midnight—to determine if the charges would be entertained. Graves, in a typical speech of unmeasured length, protested against the trial as being unscriptural. In the only vote that was not unanimous, the church rejected Graves' motion to quash the proceedings, 41 to 98.

The church employed a reporter to record the proceedings, word for word, which at the end of five more church meetings it published in a book of 112 pages. Graves also brought out a book, *Both Sides,* twice as big (240 pages), in which he carried each charge in the case and his own lengthy rebuttal. To each of the five charges the church devoted a single business session. Thus with the four introductory sessions to decide if and how the trial would be conducted, the church was in session a total of nine times from September into November, 1858—at least once for some five hours and in the entire nine perhaps as many as twenty hours.

Every vote, except that on Graves' motion to quash as indicated above, was unanimous to sustain the charge: Wednesday, October 13, to sustain the first count, 80 to 0; Friday, October 15, second count, 79 to 0; Monday, October 18, third count, 84 to 0; Tuesday, October 19, fourth count, 76 to 0; Wednesday, November 10, fifth count, 79 to 0. The final vote to expell J. R. Graves from membership in the First Baptist Church of Nashville, also on November 10, was 78 to 0. A man named Davidson who had spoken against taking such drastic action evidently abstained from the final vote.

The amount of time given to the matter gives some indication of its significance to the church. Perhaps equally important is the consistency of participation by the congregation. Over a period of some nine weeks in as many different meetings the attendance was almost exactly the same at each session.

Significance of the Issues

The two protagonists were committed in the controversy with all the remarkable intensity of their dominant persons. So, too, were those who joined them in the struggle, both those immediately in the Nashville environs and the many who became involved from afar.

Witness the mad scene at the Nashville church on the night of the beginning when strangers poured in from adjacent communities

along with members of the congregation to crowd the building.
Witness also the regularity of attendance from the congregation
through *nine* recurring church sessions.

But the true significance of the spectacle went far beyond the
personal element. The account makes the event appear to be a
personal feud between Graves and Howell—which of course it
was. Each was deeply involved personally, and that with an intensity of feeling each toward the other.

But it was much more than a personal feud.

The provocation was the total concept known as Landmarkism.
That concept challenged all other denominations at the point of
their existence, insisting that they were not true churches but only
human societies. It asked, "Will we admit that there are other
churches than Baptist?"

It posed hard positions with regard to church ordinances, insisting
upon narrow practices of baptism and the Lord's Supper. These
views and practices Landmarkers wanted to enforce at the denominational level. Denominational bodies would thus become ecclesiastical courts to sit in judgment on doctrine and practice.

These were very serious matters. True, they were not the issues
discussed directly in the controversy. But they were in the background. These issues had disturbed the fellowship, and had provoked the controversy. They were indeed significant. It would
truly be impossible to over-estimate their significance.

To the Very Extremities

Involvement of the denomination beyond the church spread
literally to the utmost extremities of the Convention. First, Graves
and his party, following the church meeting which had finally
adjourned at midnight, remained for a rump session in which they
declared that the majority of the First Church, being disorderly,
was, therefore, no true church, but that they, the minority,
(numbering twenty-three) were indeed "the true and orderly First
Baptist Church of Nashville." Not until the majority took legal
action to restrain them did the minority desist from calling themselves the First Baptist Church; they then assumed from their loca-

tion the name Spring Street Baptist Church.

Influenced by Graves, the Baptist General Association of Tennessee and North Alabama in annual session at Lebanon in the fall of 1858 (while the Graves trial was in process) refused to seat the messengers from the majority group of the Nashville church but recognized instead those that had been appointed by the minority. The following August the Concord Association took similar action, thus assuming, as Howell said, "to act as an ecclesiastical authority in seating messengers." The Association then elected Graves as moderator.

Graves also published a leaflet which indicated that he expected the Southern Baptist Convention to take similar action with regard to seating messengers from the Nashville church(es). Had his expectation been realized, the reelection of Howell to the Convention presidency would have thereby been successfully forestalled.

That the Howell-Graves controversy was an issue—almost certainly *the* issue—in the election of the Convention president in 1859 is very clear. Very likely it was a factor as early as 1857, for in that year in Louisville Howell, who had presided at the previous two biennial meetings, was not reelected on the first but on the second ballot.

Then in 1859 the excited throng assembled in Richmond—twice as many as the top number in any previous meeting. When Howell let the gavel fall to call the 580 delegates to order, the question in everyone's mind was, "Who will be elected president? Will Howell be reelected? Is Graves strong enough to oust him?"

The procedure then was to ballot without any nominations. But there had been ample campaigning—in the papers, through correspondence, by word of mouth. When the ballots were counted, for the first time in Convention annals the actual vote was recorded: "Votes cast, 434; necessary to a choice, 218; Howell, 228; Jeter, 95; Fuller, 54; Scattering, 57."

"Brethren," Howell sighed in relief, "from my heart I thank you for this renewed testimony of your continued kindness." But he insisted that there had been thrust upon the Convention matters which were the province of local church autonomy and diverted the body from its greater concerns. He said that two years before in Louisville he had determined not to preside again, but to announce that decision would be "to decline a position which probably you had no disposition to confer."

His name had become identified "with certain great principles in Church Polity" and he was determined not to allow his reelection to the presidency to divert the Convention "to questions which belong alone to our churches in their individual and sovereign capacity."

For these reasons, Howell concluded, "I beg permission, respectfully and affectionately, but firmly to resign the presidency which you have now again kindly bestowed." (For Howell's full address of resignation see the Appendix.)

At that same meeting in Richmond the Convention passed this resolution: "That, as members of this Convention, we express our earnest conviction that personal controversies among pastors, editors, and brethren, should, from this time forth, be more than ever studiously avoided."

Whereupon this motion was immediately recorded: "That the Editors of our religious papers be requested to publish the above resolution."

Still No End in Sight

That did not end the involvement of Southern Baptists. Taking account of "our serious difficulties" in "our troubled Zion," Mississippi Baptists in 1860 appointed a committee of thirteen to attempt a mediation. They also requested South Carolina Baptists to take similar steps, but without affirmative response.

When the Mississippi committee appeared in Nashville, Howell did a striking thing. He kept the committee cooling their heels, and never did see them the several days they tarried in Nashville. After they had returned to their native state, Howell wrote seven letters which he preserved in his Memorial. In these letters he spelled out with clarity and minutely the principles of church polity as an explanation of his singular aloofness. This discerning explanation of polity will claim appropriate attention in a later chapter.

Here in gist (but certainly not in jest!) it may simply be reported that Howell and his church felt fully competent to handle their own local problem without the unsolicited aid of a meddling outside committee.

Then the self-styled "true and orderly Church"—all of whom by now had been expelled along with Graves from the First Baptist Church of Nashville—invited the churches of the Concord Association to form a council to hear the evidence and reach a decision in the trial of J. R. Graves. Twenty churches of the Concord Association (not including the First Church of Nashville which made no reply) responded to the invitation of the Spring Street church. Each sent its pastor and one layman to form the council which met for three days, March 1-3, 1859, in the Odd Fellows Hall in Nashville.

The proceedings of this tribunal, reported verbatim, fill the voluminous 240 pages of *Both Sides*. The book quotes in entirety each of the five charges brought against Graves and in each instance the exhaustive defense of the meticulously overpowering defendant. Howell said that it was an ex parte tribunal called at the behest of the defendant, without authority in Baptist polity and by the nature of its origin incapable of an objective verdict. More too later on the significant aspects of polity, but even now there is no wonder that such a body would find their hero completely innocent of all charges.

Compared with Other Conflicts

Enough has now been recounted to create the inescapable impression that the Howell-Graves controversy was an engagement of considerable proportions. The immediate effect was aptly suggested in the phrase, "our troubled Zion." That "trouble" extended from Baltimore to Galveston, from Missouri to Florida. It threatened the peace and prosperity of an infant Convention.

Already the Foreign Mission Board had had to deal with I. J. Roberts, a nagging carry-over personality quirk from the Triennial era whose case ultimately was spread over 17 pages of fine print in the Convention annual (1855). Even as early as 1852 the Convention had been embarrassed by the "apostasy" of T. F. Curtis, Corresponding Secretary of the Domestic Board and one-time trusted professor of theology at the Howard.

At that moment in 1858, Crawford Howell Toy, nephew to Mrs. Howell, was in the University of Virginia engaged in his thorough season of intense training for a brilliant career of biblical teaching which would be terminated at Southern Seminary because of his doubts of the "supernatural as an element of Scripture."

In the unsuspected future lurked the then-undreamed-of Whitsitt controversy at Southern Seminary, which at its peak would threaten the continuance of a suspect institution on the moot question of Baptist succession. Because one professor candidly inquired as to the absolute actuality of uninterrupted historical Baptist continuity, Southern Baptists would be led to question an entire faculty.

Still more further removed in time was the evolution-modernism-orthodoxy melee to be championed by J. Frank Norris in the first half of the present century.

All of these would take their toll. Each in its distinctive way would be damaging, would present its trials and its frustrations.

Any attempt at comparing and contrasting the destruction, potential and actual, left in the wake of such storms is admittedly presumptious. Who can measure the dimensions of strife?

And yet in truth one can confidently assert that the controversy between R. B. C. Howell and J. R. Graves was one of the most serious Southern Baptists have ever known. It involved at the time the length and breadth, the height and depth of the entire Convention. It had in it all of the elements to threaten permanently the organized life of Southern Baptists. Its effects are still felt to this day. It just may have been the very most serious the Southern Baptist Convention has ever known.

From the measured perspective of that surmise, it is in order to probe with deliberate thoroughness the issues that provoked the contest. This search will occupy the next chapter. After that will be reviewed the meaning of the conflict. Then, in conclusion, "Polity and the President" will characterize Howell as a person and as a Southern Baptist patriarch.

11

Why the Big Fuss?

Two members of the First Baptist Church in Nashville, at a regular church meeting on September 8, 1858, charged "Rev. J. R. Graves, a member of said church and one of the editors of *The Tennessee Baptist,* with grossly immoral and unchristian conduct in four distinct cases, as follows:

> First, in that he has sought to bring upon R. B. C. Howell, the pastor of said church, reproach and injury, and thus destroy his character and influence in the Southwest, by forcing him into collision with Rev. A. C. Dayton, late corresponding secretary of the Bible Board, and now one of his [Grave's] assistant editors, through the publication in his said paper of various false and malicious representations.
>
> Secondly, In that he has endeavored to distract and divide said church, by means of a conflict between its pastor and four of its deacons, and several others of its influential members, which he has labored to produce by various inflamatory articles, published in his paper.
>
> Thirdly, In that he has uttered and published in his said paper against R. B. C. Howell, the pastor of this church, sundry foul and atrocious libels.
>
> Fourthly, In that he has at various times attacked, slandered and abused ministers and brethren of high character, belonging to our denomination, throughout the country, in his said paper.

At a later church meeting two other members charged Graves with "falsehood in nine specifications."

These five charges were the bases of consideration and decision
by the church in its nine extended sessions. Graves attended only
one of the meetings. After the church rejected his protest and refused to quash the proceedings, Graves asserted that he could not
maintain fellowship with the church because it was disorderly,
that it had rejected the plain instructions of Christ for settling disputes as recorded in Matthew 18, and he, therefore, boycotted all
further church meetings of the trial.

Thus at subsequent sessions, the defendant was never present
nor was he represented. The verbatim report of the trial is given
in the account as recorded at the time by the reporter employed by
the church. That word-for-word report was published by the
church in the book *The Trial of J. R. Graves.* Since the defendant
was neither present nor represented, the content of this record is
of course in terms of the prosecution. Although charges were
brought and signed in writing by four members of the church, the
presentation throughout is in the words of the offended, R. B. C.
Howell.

Graves claimed his turn later, at the three-day meeting in March
of the council called by the church formed from the group expelled
by First Church. The full report of that council Graves published
in the 240-page book *Both Sides.* It records meticulously each of
the five charges, followed in each instance in minute detail by
Graves' personal defence against the charge.

Denominational Relevance

There is surely no need here even to brief the voluminous details
of that intensive engagement. Each of the contestants was a
worthy exponent of his views, which he expressed fully, persuasively,
with conviction. Some aspects do need clarification. Others even
now have timely relevance.

First, the pertinence of the Bible Board and of A. C. Dayton.
That Board was the third agency of the Southern Convention, following the original two mission Boards. Located in Nashville and
directed by A. C. Dayton, it was a point of controversy for several
years and over interrelated issues. Chiefly, the unsettled questions

about the Board centered in its executive, A. C. Dayton, and his writings, chiefly his *Theodesia Ernest.* This religious novel, evidently intended to portray the writer's own pilgrimage from his earlier pedobaptist childhood to the maturity of New Testament orthodoxy, continued to have strong influence into the present century.

Meantime, Dayton had gained recognition as one of the Landmark Triumvirate—along with Graves and J. M. Pendleton. The issue of the continuance of the Bible Board was rife in 1857. As a result, Dayton lost his executive position, Howell as Convention president being party to the opposition to the Bible Board. The three Land-markers therefore plunged into fierce combat with this presumptive foe of Dayton and the Board.

A second denominational circumstance is inherent in the second charge against Graves. There had been a strong movement to establish a Southern Baptist board of publication, to carry primarily the responsibility of publishing Sunday School literature. The movement went so far as to cause a special convention to be called. It was held in the Nashville environs shortly after Howell's return (1857) to Nashville. Howell attended the meeting and gave his strong support to the idea of a board to publish Sunday School literature.

Graves was made chairman of the committee to formulate the proposal, including nomination of personnel. When Graves brought the committee report, Howell voiced strong objection on at least three scores:

1) The men named as the board of managers were not qualified theologically to select for publication Sunday School literature "for our children."

2) The proposed board would be in competition with the existing Southern Baptist Publication Society. Howell felt that support should rather be extended to strengthen the existing Society.

3) Establishment of a new board of publication in Nashville would *seem* to be designed for the personal pecuniary benefit of J. R. Graves and his Southwestern Publishing House.

It must be remembered that not only Graves and Dayton but also the others proposed by the Graves committee as the board of managers were all members of the church of which Howell was pastor. As their pastor he readily granted their business and political competency. But he also as freely insisted that they lacked theological competence to sit in judgment on material planned for the religious guidance of children. In contrast, Howell pointed to the superior theological training and experience of those who had editorial responsibility with the Publication Society in Charleston— "Basil Manly, Jr., E. T. Winkler, H. A. Tupper."

Property of the Church

The second charge against Graves asserted that he had exploited Howell's evaluation of the proposed board of managers to drive a wedge between "its pastor and four of its deacons, and several others of its influential members." His paper had been used, the charge asserted, to foment and aggravate ill feelings between pastor and leading members, by egging the members on to be offended by the pastor's frank personal appraisals.

When Graves insisted that the dispute between editor and pastor was personal and should have been settled in the personal way outlined in Matthew 18, Howell made the significant point that the pastor's influence and leadership in his congregation was not a personal matter. It was very much one of public concern.

"The fair standing and usefulness of a pastor," said Howell, "are certainly the property of the church of which he is the servant. Any attempt . . . to lessen his influence and his usefulness . . . is an offense against God, his church and his people."

Had Graves gone to his pastor privately, Howell added, "and made reliction," that would not have "atoned for his offence against the church and against brethren throughout the country."

Speaking to the church, Howell outlined church polity in dealing with one who has offended publicly by attacking the pastor and others. "The nature of the deed," he insisted, "required *public* discipline. There is no call to admonish a public offender privately before we arraign him publicly."

Howell's insistence that an attack on a pastor in its adverse effect on his ministry is of concern primarily to the church is of course valid. Even more overt and, therefore, more obvious is the public interest in slander and abuse of "ministers and brethren of his character . . . throughout the country," as asserted in the fourth charge.

In support of this charge, Howell named six men plus the Bible Board as being objects of the described assaults: Richard Fuller, pastor in Baltimore and later successor to Howell as Convention president; John Lightfoot Waller, editor in Louisville of the *Christian Repository,* charged by Graves as supporting alien immersion and open communion; William W. Everts, pastor in Louisville; William C. Duncan, editor of the *Southwestern Baptist Chronicle* and pastor in New Orleans; J. E. Dawson, pastor in Columbus, Georgia; J. P. Tustin, corresponding secretary of the Southern Baptist Publication Society, Charleston, South Carolina.

Bases of His Attacks

Typically, Graves felt it his bounden duty to attack with vigor and tenacity any instance of ministerial departure from Graves' own personal position of orthodoxy. Three of his favorite positions were with reference to nonrecognition of pedobaptist ministers, alien immersion, and close communion.

Of J. P. Tustin, Graves said that the Publication Society head was a pedobaptist in disguise, a Presbyterian at heart, and an open communionist. Graves said Tustin would welcome pedobaptist ministers to seats at conventions and would himself sit down with them at the Lord's Table if it were not for the traditional Baptist position.

Relentlessly, like a stubborn bulldog with teeth clamped on an enemy's biceps, Graves waged battle with Everts of Louisville. The offence which provoked Graves' attack: the Louisville pastor had welcomed as a visitor to his Walnut Street pulpit a Methodist minister. To Graves, Methodists and other pedobaptists had not been properly baptized, and their congregations were not true churches. Their ministers, in the absence of ordination by a true New Testament church, should never be recognized as ordained ministers of the gospel. To invite a pedobaptist minister into a Baptist pulpit to Graves was unorthodoxy of the worst sort.

Graves took the position that valid baptism brought together a proper candidate, the right purpose, the right method, *and* the authority of a New Testament church. To Graves, pedobaptists met no one of these conditions. And the Lord's Supper, being a church ordinance, could be properly observed only by the members of a local church congregation; even fellow visiting Baptists should not be invited to the table. Graves pointed out that the Southern Baptist Convention had no scriptural grounds for observing the memorial meal at its annual session. It was largely through his influence that the practice was discontinued, both at the Convention and in associational meetings.

Graves was quick to the defense of these views wherever any deviation appeared, whether expressed by a fellow editor or by any leading pastor. More will be said in the next chapter about the nature of his attacks. Right here it is well to remark that the fourth charge brought against Graves in the Nashville church was not directed against the doctrinal position so much as it was against the spirit of those attacks.

One exception as to provocation of a Graves attack upon a prominent brother was his published "slander" of Richard Fuller. In his paper Graves reported that at a recent meeting Fuller had spoken *seven* times. It is quite understandable that a man like Graves who was accustomed to speaking *three hours* on a stretch would be offended at any competitor who claimed the floor so often!

In the "specifications" on the fourth charge Howell named and described slander and abuse of six men. He said he could have named "Crowell, Crane, Bestor, Chambless, Teasdale, Tichenor, Henderson, Taliaferro, Manly, Kendrick, Hillsman, Coleman, Lynd, Caldwell, Branan, Tyler, Dagg, Mell and others." Add them up and you get a total of eighteen. And when you consult their addresses you will discover that they resided in at least seven different states. Quite an array of opponents against whom Graves had whetted his sword!

"Aegis of Our Protection"

The sting of that venom, Howell said, imposed a clear duty upon the church. To his congregation and against one of his own members the pastor pled: "*A most solemn duty rests upon you.* Brethren in every quarter of the land have felt his blows. They have appealed to you for protection against his defamatory attacks." These appeals had come from "Duncan of Louisiana, Crane of Mississippi, Tustin of South Carolina, Coleman of Arkansas, Everts of Kentucky."

Failure to act now, Howell pointed out, would by default lend church support and encouragement to Graves virulence. "The aegis of our protection," he said, "has been upon him [Graves]. Brethren have appealed to us for protection against him—from Kentucky, Louisiana, Missouri, Arkansas, Mississippi, Alabama, South Carolina, Georgia. They could reach Graves only through us. We were their only defence. His public shame was settling upon us." The pastor insisted that the church could no longer be silent.

Graves' immediate response when the church refused his motion to quash the proceedings was to announce that he could no longer have fellowship with the church because scriptural uses of Matthew 18 had not been followed.

"I withdraw from the church!" he said dramatically. It was now approaching the midnight hour, the church meeting having been in session for some four hours.

The moderator, a discerning layman named Winston, reminded Graves that by church polity a person could cease being a church member only by death or by exclusion. Graves replied that "when a majority of a church tramples upon the law of Christ they become a faction and are no longer a church." If the church proceeded, Graves said he would "be no party, direct or indirect, to such unscriptural proceedings." On this basis he and his minority said that they were the "true and orderly First Baptist Church of Nashville."

The Graves Defence

Graves did not attend another of the nine sessions of his trial by the church. Rather, he made his detailed defence the following

March before the special council which was called by the newly formed church composed of his party. He declared that "Howell and Hillsman [a Knoxville editor] have declared a war against their Landmark brethren and that they [the Landmark brethren] are to be proscribed from the Boards that direct the great interests of Southern Baptists."

The attack by Howell was "surprising and shocking." This attack was in Howell's letter published in *The Christian Index,* in which he opposed the proposed Southern Baptist Sunday School Union because "we already had the Southern Baptist Publication Society in Charleston which had the same objects."

Graves had been the chairman of the committee to draw up specifications for the proposed Union, which Union Howell sought to defeat. "The men nominated," said Graves in defence of those he had named and whom Howell asserted in his *Index* letter lacked the requisite theological competence, "are the best qualified on deciding the character of books best suited to children and youth."

Howell's frank appraisal of that lack, as stated in his *Index* letter, Graves said was "an attempt to tear asunder the body of Christ, the integrity and harmony of which he is under the most sacred obligations to seek by every means in his power." Graves charged that Howell had made "repeated and persevering attacks upon the union and integrity of this church" and thereby had provoked "public protracted and violent agitation to divide and overthrow and destroy this church."

In his book, *Both Sides,* Graves is reported as reading before the council many letters, from J. B. Jeter (Va.), Richard Fuller (Md.), W. C. Buck (Ala.), Judge Stocks (Ga.) and others refuting the charge of slander against prominent brethren and giving personal opinions on dealing with differences as instructed by Christ in Matthew 18.

The aim of Howell and of his church leaders was accomplished when Graves was unanimously expelled from the church. This was evidently a secondary aim. The primary purpose is suggested in a letter received by Howell during the trial.

At one of the church meetings Howell read a paragraph from a letter he had just received, saying it was the talk at the meeting of

the Liberty Association that Howell had been paid $1500 by pedo-
baptists to "ruin Graves as a preacher and his veracity as a man."

Almost certainly this talk was no more than a rumor, although
pedobaptists would have delighted to see that end achieved. Howell,
too, and his associates were not so much interested in expelling
Graves from the church as they were in the effect their action would
have on Graves' influence.

Nor can the reader of history give total credence to what combatants themselves say as to the cause of their conflict. One must
plow deeper than the explanations of Howell and Graves for a true
understanding of why they were fussing.

The Unspoken Causes

The causes of any conflict are always hidden in the complexities
of enigmatic human nature. In any debate, opponents are ever
hesitant to confront the central issue. Rather, they sidestep the
real point of difference and divert attention to incidentals. This
diversionary tactic prevails whether in Congress, in a town council,
or in a church conference.

For instance, when Jesus asked his disciples what they had been
arguing about along the way (Mark 9:33,34), every last one of them
was immediately mum. They would not—perhaps *could* not—put
in words an admission of the embarrassing contention. Their closed
mouths illustrate our characteristic unwillingness to admit the personal factor which always is present in any heated conflict.

In debate that raises a high temperature, there are always personal
explanations, but these cannot be taken at face value. They will be
diversionary. The real reasons must be found beneath the surface.
The more intense the conflict, the greater the inner compulsion of
the contestants to offer incidental personal reasons for the conflict.
Their own language affords no more than a starter toward understanding the real provocations.

Both Howell and Graves had much to say as to the causes of the
conflict which rocked a denomination. Howell complained of slander
and abuse, of recurring efforts to foment dissatisfaction with his
pastoral leadership. There was conclusive evidence to support the

veracity of these charges, but also without doubt there were earlier causes to provoke the abuse.

Each said that the conflict started over disagreement over the proposed Southern Baptist Sunday School Union. But this mutual acknowledgment leaves unanswered the question as to *why* the one opposed the proposal which the other championed. Why would one—*anyone*—oppose the publication of Sunday School literature, materials for the study of the Bible? Who would oppose *this* Union?

Really, it was not opposition to publication nor to *this* Union that was a primary cause of the conflict. Rather, it was opposition to a man and to his dominant nature. The elaboration of this thesis will occupy the entire next chapter—namely, that the church and the pastor in the many tedious and trying hours of trial aimed not at a man personally but at a deep-seated spirit of dogmatic assertiveness which could never be tolerated in a spiritual democracy. It had to be exorcised. The only answer was complete eradication.

If the pedobaptists wanted to "ruin Graves as a pracher and his veracity as a man," Howell just as devoutly set himself to the intense purpose of defeating the self-aggrandized arrogance of a man who always claimed that he was right and everyone else was wrong.

Their Relative Positions

One further word as to why their big fuss. This has to do with their relative positions, before 1850 and after Howell's return to Nashville in 1857. You see, Howell for half a generation—from 1835 until his departure for Richmond in 1850—was the acknowledged spokesman for Baptists in the Great Valley. He assumed that position when he came, commission in hand from the Mission Board in Philadelphia and a call from the strategic albeit struggling congregation in the gateway town on the Cumberland.

Immediately, he established *The Baptist.* At once it was the organ of communication and the predominant influence throughout the denomination in the Southwest. His was a position of trust, of leadership, of prominence until the day he left. And even after he had taken up residence in Richmond, it was in a meeting at Nashville that Southern Baptists elected him to preside in triennial session—and then again and again and again, biennially, in Montgomery, in Baltimore, in Louisville.

Howell was implored in 1857 to return to the Nashville pastorate—and presumably to his former place of regional denominational leadership—and he acceded to the plea almost surely in considerable measure because of the inroads of a reactionary Landmarkism.

Like the king in the fable who returned home to find another occupying his throne, Howell returned to find another entrenched in favor. Howell himself in another context points out that Graves at the time was "the acknowledged champion of the church throughout the Southwest and his influence and power were felt throughout the whole country."

It must be remembered that Howell at the outset had himself put Graves on the road that led to influence and prominence. He had selected and named as associate editor back in 1845 the young schoolteacher who had drifted in to Nashville from Vermont by way of Kentucky. And now the returned Convention president and denominational statesman found this young upstart occupying the identical spot formerly locked in the grasp of the old patriarch.

The disparity in their age added emotional fervor to their ultimate and inevitable conflict. Howell in 1858 was fifty-seven years old—that at a time when life expectancy was much less than his "advanced" years. A man who had lived more than half a century expected to receive due veneration. In contrast, Graves was only thirty-eight—old enough to feel his maturity, but still relatively to the older man hardly in the same patriarchal class.

The inevitable clash became a contest between age and youth, between the wisdom of many years and the brashness of inexperience. It was intensified by the aggravation to an elder in being replaced by the younger. The personal circumstances had all of the conditions to add fuel to the flame.

But there were deeper meanings to the conflict which now claim our most serious attention in the following chapter.

12

The Meaning of the Conflict

"This case," Howell said to his church in business meeting in September 1858, "will test the polity of our churches. It will either destroy or establish it."

In similar vein, J. R. Graves the following March spoke in "Gratitude that the laws of our land and the genius of our church polity allow me to speak for and defend myself."

The two had widely differing purposes in mind, and their rationalizations on church polity were poles apart, but the two opponents agreed that the key factor in their dispute was the essential of church polity. The relevance of polity is assuredly inherent to an understanding of the meaning of their conflict.

Strangely, at the outset their views on church polity were essentially the same. In the heat of battle Graves altered his position under the personal mandate of self-preservation.

"You and only you," Howell insisted to his church, "are the judges, and the scriptural judges, of the law and the facts." When the church speaks, he said, there is no appeal. The judgment of the church is final. Even when a church expels a member the only way of restoration is through the renewal of fellowship by the *expelling church*.

"Can an expelled person join some church other than the one that expelled him?" Howell asked. His answer was no. "To do so," he pointed out, "injures the expelled member. It makes insoluble the conflict between him and the church. It hurts the fellowship of churches. It creates war between churches. It overthrows healthful discipline. You then have no discipline that you can enforce."

If a member is unjustly expelled, Howell said that the remedy is in "earnest, heartfelt, fervent, humble religion." In a word, he said that it was love. Church membership, he insisted, is not to be taken lightly; the doors of the church are to be guarded with diligence against the unworthy. The ample remedy for the member expelled he said is the church itself: "Its doors are always open to him."

On Church Authority

In these positive statements Howell was refuting the position Graves had taken after his expulsion. He was also confirming Graves' own earlier published stand.

As late as October 6, 1857 (his trial before the church was twelve months later), "Baptist Correllaries" appeared in *The Tennessee Baptist,* one of them being: "That a body of immersed believers is the highest ecclesiastical authority in the world, and the only tribunal for the trial of cases of discipline; that the acts of the church are of superior binding force over those of an association, convention, council, or presbytery—and no association or convention can impose a moral obligation upon the constituent parts composing them. J. R. Graves, Editor."

This was Graves' polity statement before he himself was brought into personal collision with that "highest ecclesiastical authority." He published the "Correllaries" repeatedly in his paper as a sort of platform statement. But his actions when he had been expelled belied his own statement of polity. *Then* he denied ultimate church authority on the ground that the church action was not in accord with the teaching of Christ in Matthew 18, announced his personal withdrawal from the church, and set up another church which called Graves as pastor.

In painful retrospect, Howell recalled that twenty-five years earlier Alexander Campbell had been expelled. Refusing to accept the expulsion, Campbell had appealed to churches and the associations. They had sustained him, and thus was born the schism of Campbellism.

The parallel was painfully obvious. Refusing to accept the verdict
of the church, Graves had not only erected another church amenable
to his views but had also used that church to call a council—Howell
called it an ex parte council—as a superior authority to hear the
evidence and overrule the decision of the church in the trial of
J. R. Graves.

In effect Howell charged Graves with rejecting church discipline
and authority. It was through this abridgement of church authority—
or the compromise of church polity—that Landmarkism was being
entrenched.

Howell rejected that abridgement of church polity. He did so in
speeches at the church meetings.

One member of the congregation, a man named Davidson, spoke
against the inevitable church action. He "had now no doubt that
the church would expel Graves; it would be folly to say anything in
the hope of averting it." Rather his concern was for the effect:
"Neither Dr. Howell nor Mr. Graves will out-live the evil consequence
to the Baptist Convention of this trial." For this reason Davidson
"deeply regretted the action of the church."

In reply, Howell spoke at length on church polity in dealing with
one who has offended publicly by attacking the pastor and others.
The nature of the church, said the pastor, required public discipline.
There was no call to admonish a public offender privately before he
had been arraigned publicly.

Limit of Denominational Power

Then moving to dissertation on denominational structure, Howell
said that councils had come to be regarded—"as associations already
are in this part of the country"—as a sort of tribunal, outside of the
church (and above them), and possessed of original jurisdiction.

The only organizations recognized in the divine order, said Howell,
are churches—"each independent, recognizing no sovereign but
Christ." Their union with each other "is indirect and dependent on
their union with Christ."

Their authority is "delegated by Christ. Delegated authority cannot be redelegated to another. To do so violates the primary

authority. Churches cannot delegate authority to councils or associations. Councils have no original authority. They cannot decide
for a church any *matter of discipline,* even though a church desires
it. The church must itself speak, or no authoritative decision is
ever pronounced. From the decision of the church there is no appeal. It is final."

The natural tendency Howell admitted is to lodge power with
councils. It is toward ecclesiastical despotism, toward popery and
council. For this reason proper guards must be thrown around the
church. It was at this point that Howell exclaimed: "This case
will test the polity of our churches. It will either destroy or establish it." The test to which he alluded is at the point of the autonomy of the churches.

That the trial did indeed become such a test Howell later pointed
out in his letters to the Mississippi committee which had sought to
intervene in the hopes of achieving a reconciliation. Howell, you
remember, would not even see the committee when they came all
the way from Mississippi to Nashville and requested a meeting.
Neither Howell nor his own church committee would grant this
direct approach.

Nor had either solicited help. The point at issue said Howell was
between the church and J. R. Graves. In line with the cardinal
polity principle of church autonomy, the church was well able to
manage its own affairs. Indeed the church had already settled the
issue the previous fall, the visit by the Mississippi committee in
Nashville being two years later, in the summer of 1860.

And, Howell added, if the church had consulted with any one
it would not have sought it from a "mere missionary society such
as the Baptist State Convention of Mississippi."

Thus, the polity-conscious Howell made clear that the supreme
test of the case involved a clear grasp of church autonomy and just
as definitely an acceptance of its attendant limitation of denominational authority. If a church is to be free and independent, no
denominational body can be allowed to exercise a countermanding
overlordship.

As early as 1835, Howell in *The Baptist* had voiced his concern

that associations showed a definite trend toward becoming "ecclesiastical courts." This alarm he expressed repeatedly. And his
reference to "a mere missionary society" was most certainly not
limited to the Mississippi Convention. The phrase appears often,
always in a deliberate tone to play down the authority of a denominational body. To Howell, the Southern Baptist Convention of
which he was president was merely a missionary society. It had no
primary authority over the churches.

To the Mississippi committee, after their return, Howell wrote:
"The church never had admitted, it never will admit the right of
your Convention, or any other convention, association council,
or similar organization to interfere in any case of discipline which
may occur in its own body."

Trouble came, said Howell, when an association turned from
being "a mere missionary society" and overreached its authority.
"Most unfortunate," he said of one association, "was in the powers
it gradually assumed." It claimed jurisdiction over the churches
and this "led to its overthrow."

It was exactly this extension of power that Graves cultivated
when his new church of the minority called an associational council
to overrule his own trial by the Nashville church. Also, the Concord
Association, evidently influenced by Graves, in 1858 while the
Graves trial was in process censured the Nashville church for its
handling of the Graves case, and the next year would not seat the
First church delegates but seated rather the delegates from the
Graves church and elected Graves as moderator.

It was against the assumption of such ecclesiastical powers as these
that Howell complained as being "most unfortunate." Presumably
Graves hoped in 1859 to exercise similar influence over the Southern
Baptist Convention; his ultimate victory would come in the refusal
of the Convention to seat First church delegates while at the same
time receiving the delegates from Graves' church.

What Is an Association?

Back in October, 1844, before Graves came to Nashvile and while
Howell was the sole editor, *The Baptist* published an answer to the

question, What is an Association? In some detail the editor replied:

> It is a union of churches in a district or a state to counsel, aid and cooperate with each other in the great work for which churches are organized. Their origin was in Palestine fifteen years after the Ascension (Acts 15; 2 Cor. 8:18 ff.).
>
> They were, and are, not for government, for legislation, or to rule in any sense, but simply to act in cooperation for the spread of the Gospel. They have no permanent officers, their organization is the simplest possible, and their work is purely executive—to carry out the will of Christ respecting the preaching of the Gospel.
>
> Associations are formed of delegates or 'messengers' from churches—not of representatives, for the churches themselves are representatives of Christ. Nor is it supposed that the churches delegate to them *all* their own authority. . . . We recognize no lawgiver but Christ and no government but His. Should the churches authorize the Association to make laws or to govern them they would thereby put the Association in the place of Christ; and were they to assume this authority over the churches they would thereby usurp the authority of Christ. The churches then are the supreme authority and the associations are necessarily inferior and subordinate, the creatures of the churches—auxiliary bodies, designed merely to counsel, and arrange for efficient action. They subserve the purpose of the churches.
>
> By a combination of their moral strength (they) are able to pursue some of their objects with greater energy, and to prosecute them to a greater extent than they could do without such annual consultation. These objects are to send ministers to the destitute, to aid feeble churches, to send the Bible to the ignorant—in a word, to use all the means God has placed in our hands to subjugate man, at home and abroad, to the dominion of Christ. In an association, knowledge is possessed by persons present of conditions throughout the territory, mutual counsels will lead to prudent and concerted action, the little energy of each church, which would not by itself be effective, when

thrown together forms a reservoir of power. These counsels
produce acquaintance, destroy jealousies, create sympathy
and love, and produce mutual cooperation, prayers and labors.
This is pleasing to God, is according to His Word, and con-
sequently has received and will continue to receive His blessing.

To his church at the Graves trial in 1858 Howell said that "the
violation of these principles by our association"—the infringement
by the association on the autonomy of the church—"has been the
fruitful source of nearly all the contentions, agitations, and schisms
with which Tennessee has been rife since the first settlement of the
country."

What schism in forty years, he asked, had not been concocted and
set in motion by associations? By overstepping their authority and
imposing their ecclesiastical will on the churches, he charged that
the associations had fomented division in the churches. All were
due he said to "flagrant violations of the principle of church autonomy."

"You will never surrender your independent authority," Howell
said confidently to his congregation. In his Memorial, Howell reported that Graves had published a pamphlet designed to influence
the Southern Baptist Convention in 1859 in the same way he influenced the General Association (of Tennessee and North Alabama)
and the Concord Association. This pamphlet had been enlarged
into a book of 240 pages and advertised for everyone (evidently the
reference is to *Both Sides*).

Howell deplored the adverse effect from the Graves faction. In
five years the total membership of the churches in the Concord
Association had declined by 882. The most withering effect had
been on contributions; in one recent quarter Howell reported that
the total for missions from all of Tennessee had been only $39.70.

By the Ablest Men

But he was glad to note some good from the contest. The Graves
controversy, Howell pointed out, "has caused intense interest in
church government." The subject had been "thoroughly discussed

by the ablest men."

Graves himself had elicited the discussion by propounding central questions to representative Convention persons—P. H. Mell of Georgia, Richard Fuller of Maryland, J. B. Jeter of Virginia. Their replies to his questions Graves published in *The Tennessee Baptist* and in *Both Sides.* The questions: What is the Christian duty for settling a disagreement as taught by Christ in Matthew 18? What is the church's responsibility with respect to Christ's teachings? When a church does not observe these rules and flagrantly expels a member, what is now his duty? What right of appeal does he have to a council or higher tribunal? How can the expelled member be restored to church membership?

These are typical of the key questions on church government that were discussed "by the ablest men." In spite of all the pain the trial had caused him—so much that "all the afflictions of my life put together would not amount to a tenth of the sufferings from this trial"—Howell could still be glad for its beneficent focus on church polity.

Indeed, that focus is a positive value from the heated controversy. It accomplished a hearty discussion—frank, bold, unrestrained. Very certainly, difference of opinion may be tolerated when men are free to express those differences. Even more, difference of opinion freely expressed is much beyond an allowable tolerance; it has inherent value. Honest debate, freely contested, is of great worth in reaching valid community judgment.

The freedom of expression enjoyed by both Graves and Howell, tolerated at the time by a community with the wholesome capacity for hearing "both sides," was the lively mark of a society removed no more than two generations from the independent frontier. Both contestants relied as a lifelong commitment upon the printed page for the communication of their views. Moreover, the site of their contest was Nashville, then as now an acknowledged center of printed communications.

A Vigorous Press

Historically, communication by printing is a major Nashville phenomenon. Even from the early settlement on the banks of the Cumberland, Nashville has been noted as a printing center. The first printing press in the state was brought on horseback in 1791 by George Roulstone from Fayetteville, North Carolina. A decade later, some Bradfords and one John McLaughlin brought presses to Nashville and established the first newspapers on the Cumberland.

After 1820, there were many pamphlets and books on religion, politics, agriculture, science published and sold in Nashville. Almanacs and minutes of the Concord Association were published annually. By 1850, according to Davenport in *Cultural Life in Nashville on the Eve of the Civil War,* Nashville was recognized as one of the important publishing centers in the nation. J. H. Sears, in *Tennessee Printers 1791-1945,* says it was "a land where every man had his own ideas and was anxious to spread them among his neighbors."

The biggest single addition at one time to the printing industry in Nashville was the coming of the Methodist Publishing House in 1854, four years before the eruption of the Howell-Graves controversy. When Methodists, like Baptists, divided over the slave question in 1845, ownership of their publishing house, then located in Philadelphia, provoked legal turmoil which was finally settled in Nashville, bringing their book manufacturing and book bindery, equipment and people from Philadelphia.

The Howell-Graves episode embroiled the Nashville community more intensely and drew the lines of strong personality differences more sharply and, thereby, pointed up the reliance on popular media of communication more definitely than any previous event in the development of the printing industry in Nashville.

The relation of the conflict to the printing industry in Nashville is surely apparent. Graves and his forces had at their disposal *The Tennessee Baptist* which, according to Howell, "in their hands is an engine of great power," with its circulation of 12,000 readers throughout the Southwest. They also controlled a printing plant.

In contrast, wrote Howell, "The church was dumb. It had no

medium through which it could speak to the public." Thus he realized that "a weekly paper was an imperative necessity." Upon the pastor's recommendation, the church authorized the publication of the *Baptist Standard.* The first issue appeared November 10, 1858, and the paper was continued for two years with "subscribers throughout the whole South" until war forced its suspension.

The point here is plain and direct: Men always in every era are impelled with great force to express great ideas. They will not be suppressed. They must come out with deep convictions, driving concepts, whether of the spirit, or in science, or in politics, or in the arena of economics.

The most devastating emotional circumstance of all is to bottle up one's feelings, one's ideas, one's sincere thoughts. The person who holds himself in, who always suppresses and never expresses, ultimately will explode.

There are, fortunately, men in every generation like Graves and Howell who are little inclined toward suppression. They come out with it. They will find an outlet, from some platform. Society, and history, are the richer for it.

Too, it must be admitted that men of such spirit will disagree. This is inescapable, in view of the varieties of human personality. But disagreement too can be a blessing—not painful controversy, necessarily, but the leveling influence of honest differences bravely and forcefully set forth. That would be a drab and fruitless social milieu indeed, where an innocuous uniformity prevailed.

In no society of human persons can unanimous agreement ever prevail. It would be tragic if it did. Inexpressibly more tragic would be the suppression of expression—if for instance men lacked the technical know-how to communicate, or if some awful power, political or otherwise, restrained communication.

These gifts—technology, economy, intellectuality, a responsive audience, and, above all, freedom to think and to speak—are at once the causes and the opportunities in the freedom of expression which marked the Howell-Graves controversy.

A vigorous press is vital to social development and to religious progress. The blessing of such a press on the banks of the Cumber-

land, even in 1858, was becoming the wonder and the admiration
of a nation. It is illustrative of man's imperative need to be vocal—
and also of the genius operating in the larger community in development of the requisite techniques to publish that vocalization.

What Is Landmarkism?

Reference has been made to Landmarkism without as yet any
attempt to define the term. Even now such an attempt will not be
made, for a painstaking definition of the complex movement is outside the present purpose.

J. R. Graves was indeed the personification of Landmarkism. It
would be close to reality to call the movement Gravesism rather
than Landmarkism. He was the spokesman. J. M. Pendleton first
spoke of the old Landmarks in his famous pamphlet which Graves
published in 1854. A. C. Dayton was another lieutenant. The three,
Grayes, Pendleton, and Dayton, formed the widely acknowledged
Landmark triumvirate.

But it was Graves who stood at the center, in the spotlight. For
forty years Graves was the identified Landmark spokesman. He
defined Landmark in what is known as his Cotton Grove statement,
named from a place in West Tennessee where Graves addressed Baptists on June 24, 1851:

> Can Baptists, consistently with their principles or the Scrip-
> tures, recognize those societies not organized according to the
> pattern of the Jerusalem Church, but possessing different
> *governments,* different *officers,* a different class of *members,*
> different *ordinances, doctrines* and *practices,* as churches of
> Christ?
>
> Ought they to be called gospel churches, or churches in a
> religious sense?
>
> Can we consistently recognize the ministers of such irregular
> and unscriptural bodies as gospel ministers?
>
> Is it not virtually recognizing them as official ministers to
> invite them into our pulpits, or *by any other act that would
> or could be* construed into such a recognition?

> Can we consistently address as *brethren* those professing
> Christianity who not only have not the doctrine of Christ
> and walk not according to his commandments, but are
> arrayed in direct and bitter opposition to them?

Graves wrote later, in his book *Old Landmarkism: What Is It?:*
"These queries were unanimously answered in the negative and the
Baptists of Tennessee generally, and multitudes all over the South,
indorsed the decision.

"The name of Old Landmarkers came in this way. In 1854, J. M.
Pendleton, of Kentucky, wrote an essay upon this question at my
special request, viz: "Ought Baptists to recognize Pedobaptist
preachers as gospel ministers?" which I brought out in tract form,
and gave it the title, "An Old Landmark Reset." This calm discussion, which had an immense circulation in the South, was reviewed by many of the leading writers, North and South, and they,
by way of reproach, called all Baptists "Old Landmarkers" who
accepted his conclusions."

To know what Landmark is one must understand J. R. Graves—
the complexity of his personality, his primary commitments, the
nature of the man, the paradoxical vagaries of his self-defeating
inconsistencies, his hide-bound dogmatic literalism. To know Graves
is to understand Landmarkism, and to understand the two is required to know the meaning of the Howell-Graves controversy.

An apt illustration of all these interrelated complexities is Brownlow's earlier examination of the dimensions of the man Graves—
of his "convexity and concavity" when the Methodist politician
came to the logical conclusion that "he is a very little man." Another analyst, viewing Graves from another perspective, could
just as logically conclude that he was a very big man.

The thing that irritated Brownlow was Graves' assertion in *The
Great Iron Wheel* that Methodism was a human society, not a
church at all but wholly developed and perpetuated by human de-
vice. On that bold and infuriating assertion, Graves contended
relentlessly that Methodist ministers, having been ordained by a
human society and not by a true church, should never be recognized nor admitted to a Baptist pulpit.

That spirit Graves and his fellow Landmarkers sought to enforce—and did so with considerable success—in every Baptist gathering, in churches, associations, conventions. All pedobaptist ministers were suspect to the Landmarkers. And any fellow Baptist who welcomed to his pulpit a pedobaptist minister was even more suspect. It was on that basis that Graves used the columns of *The Tennessee Baptist* to attack the pastor of the Walnut Street Baptist Church in Louisville. The Louisville pastor had not only recognized a minister who had no ordination except by a human society, but had him preach in his pulpit!

This question of recognition of ministers of other denominations came up repeatedly for controversial consideration in the early biennial sessions of the Southern Baptist Convention. At the sessions in Montgomery in 1855 it was before the Convention *seven* times, with as many different motions, debates, and actions. In Richmond in 1859 action on seating "ministering brethren" was taken by the Convention five different times.

In similar contention Graves argued for his own personal position on baptism, as to mode, purpose, authority. When his own mother, who had been immersed but in a pedobaptist church, twenty years before, presented herself for membership in the church of which Graves was pastor, he would deviate not one whit from his established position. Graves required his mother to be baptized again.

Similar rigidity he applied also to the Lord's Supper—close communion of the closest sort, limited not just to those of like fellowship, but to those who were members of the local congregation which administered the ordinance. It should never be observed by a convention or an association.

But the spirit of the Landmarker ran deeper than the narrowness of doctrine. True, the doctrine was narrow. And the Landmarker held it with steadfast determination. It also lay in the distilled essence of ecclesiastics. It governed church polity with the sharpest delineation.

The Way Graves Talked

But the point of provocation in the Howell-Graves conflict—or in any other denominational clash—was sparked neither by difference of doctrine, nor by objection to ecclesiology, nor primarily by contention as to polity.

Howell disavowed the element of Landmark doctrine as causing the debate. One is obliged to conclude that the provocation to controversy was not so much in what Graves said as *in the way* he said it.

Here was a man who brazenly went to Louisville and accused a leading pastor of unorthodoxy. He repeated the irritating pattern in Columbus, Georgia, in Charleston, in New Orleans, in Baltimore, in Richmond. Is it any wonder that he stirred up deepest animosity? Those he incensed might even agree with his basic doctrines, but they could not tolerate his contentious accusations.

In the midst of their conflict Howell charged that Graves' purpose was "carried forward by men from abroad." Speaking of the postmidnight meeting when charges were brought against Graves, Howell named five men who came in to dominate the discussion. "They were thrust upon us uninvited," he said, referring to these five and to a throng of others, "to aid this faction in our disorganization and what they hoped would be our destruction. Upon such a scene as that, the sun should never shine. They supplanted the church. They replaced it. They took over."

Graves contended, and rightly, that the church should "be governed in all things by the laws of Christ." But he also just as vociferously pronounced the Nashville church to have disobeyed the law of Christ in Matthew 18. On this basis he would not personally recognize the Nashville church as a true church. On the same basis of what he termed disobedience to the laws of Christ, he would not recognize the churches of other denominations. To him they were human societies because they were not obedient in every point to his personal understanding of the laws of Christ. In effect, he insisted upon obedience to the laws as interpreted by J. R. Graves. He made himself the final judge of orthodoxy.

The Authoritarian Spirit

This was the Landmark spirit—not doctrine, not ecclesiology, not even polity, but a rigid authoritarianism which brooks no deviation from the personal literalism of its dogmatic proponent. It was a cocksure certainty by which this strongwilled Landmarker set himself up as the sole interpreter of the law and the gospel. It was an overextended assurance, individual and personal, that he himself was possessed of the truth, and that it was his duty to correct any error which he perceived in others. This early Landmarker was convinced that he alone understood the doctrine. Possessed of this knowledge, he was duty-bound to set everyone else straight.

The limit to which this malicious self-deception drove Graves brought the man and his pastor into collision that shook the Convention. Its effect continues to this day, and its presence, as men are still human, persists.

One further point warrants elaboration: the destructive effect of such a wilful spirit on the pastor's leadership and the public stake in that leadership. The second charge against Graves, remember, was that "he has endeavored to distract and divide said church by means of a conflict between its pastor and four of its deacons, and several others of its influential members."

Graves protested the trial, saying that it was a personal matter between Howell and Graves which should have been settled privately according to the law of Christ laid down in Matthew 18.

"The fair standing and usefulness of a pastor," countered Howell, "are certainly the property of the church of which he is the servant. Any attempt . . . to lessen his influence and his usefulness . . . is an offense against God, his church, and his people."

Had Graves gone to the pastor privately to make reconciliation, Howell said, this would not have "atoned for his offence against the church and against brethren throughout the country."

Howell's Contemporary Appraisal

Howell had seen enough to convince him that "the Landmark is destructive among us of all the best interests of religion." Writing in his Memorial in 1862 he summarized his own understanding at the time of the movement and of its effect in ten brief years.

Those who receive its principles are inflated by them into pride and selfishness and thus most seriously injured. They injure those upon whom attempts are made to impose their Landmark by initiating them, and destroying their brotherly love, and Christian enjoyment. They injure us all by destroying our spirituality on the one hand, and on the other by calling our thoughts perpetually to formalities, churchism, and externals generally. They cut off our approach to our erring brethren of other denominations and completely frustrate all our attempts to lead them in the scriptural paths of truth and duty. Their appearance of illiberality takes away from us the sympathy of intelligent men of the world, and thus closes against us the door of usefulness. These are enormous evils, but they are the least of those with which the Landmark has afflicted us.

The labors of our ministry have, as we saw in the last chapter, ceased in this quarter to produce any salutary results. And what effect has the Landmark had upon our denominational schools, male and female, in Middle Tennessee, and North Alabama? Ten years since we had many, and they were all prosperous. Where are they now? Except a female school at Winchester, belonging to Z. E. Graves, a brother of J. R. Graves, a pet of the reformers, and specially of the Tennessee Baptists. They have all gone down. Not one of them remains. Even Union University [Not to be confused with the present Union University in Jackson, Tennessee, which was established in 1874 as a continuation of West Tennessee College. Union University in Murfreesboro was begun in 1848 and was closed in 1861.], which they had completely subsidized to their purposes is no more. It sleeps the sleep of death. It may be said that the war had much to do in destroying these schools It had something to do with destroying the Female Academy in Murfreesborough, and the Burnett College, but Union University was hopelessly bankrupt and breathing its last when the war came, and could have existed, under any circumstances only a few months longer. The others were all overthrown before the war commenced. The Landmark destroyed them.

And where are our pastors, the men of cultivation, piety, and influence in Middle Tennessee? We have seen in a former chapter that they are all gone. Not a single man of weight, or power out of the city of Nashville remains; nor are their places supplied, or likely to be supplied. The whole field is now utterly abandoned to the Landmarkers. And not a few of them, forsaken by their congregations, and starved out by their churches have followed those whom they had before driven from the country.

At Lebanon in 1858, our missionary organizations were broken up and destroyed, since which time not fifty dollars have been contributed by all the Landmarkers in Middle Tennessee to any of the purposes of the Southern Baptist Convention. Indeed as a body they have become hostile to the Convention. In 1859 the Concord Association took measures to divide the churches, and fully consummated the schism which had been forming itself for eight, or ten years.

Thus have we seen that the Landmark, while it is impracticable, false and unscriptural is utterly destructive of all the true interests of the religion of Christ. Unhappily the truth of all this is but too deeply impressed upon us by the terrible desolations that now surround us on every side. Ten years ago the garden of the Lord was blooming and beautiful. Now it is a solitary wilderness. The only verdant spot is the city of Nashville, in which, notwithstanding the residence here of Mr. Graves, Landmarkism never had any influence.

But enough and too much of this "Old Landmark Reset." It had its origin in false doctrine, selfish purposes, and bad logic. Yet its friends would persuade us that in its advocacy they believe themselves doing God's service. And so did Saul of Tarsus, when he was persecuting the people of God, and making havoc of his churches. Desolation has followed the steps of the Landmarkers, wherever they have gone. What is to be the result in future years? God only knows. Whether it is to expire in the storm of civil war that now overwhelms us, or whether when that is passed away, it is to go on in its blighting career, the future only can reveal. Baptists in Tennessee have been ever since the state was settled, the easy victims of religious demagogues. First they were agitated, and divided on the doctrine of Divine Sovereignty; then on the doctrine of Parker; next came Campbellism; then missions; and now Landmarkism! Storm after storm has swept over the churches in quick succession. Any, it seems, who can get up a novelty and has sufficient unscrupulousness, can lash our people into a fury. When shall we have wisdom and piety enough to resist successfully these endless innovations? For ourselves, we protest that we are not Antinomian Baptists, nor Free Will Baptists, nor Old School Baptists, nor Campbellite Baptists, nor Landmark Baptists, but what we have ever been Baptists of the old apostolic stamp, taking the Bible as our exclusive guide, loving all who love Christ and ready always to do what we can to reclaim the erring and to save the lost. The treatment proper for Pedobaptist preachers, may, as we believe, be safely left to the churches, where it of right belongs, and when after all it must be left under the guidance of the word and Spirit of God. These churches may err on the side of a mistaken charity; they may precipitate themselves into a proscriptive bigotry, but a praying Christian heart will by the grace of God, eventually lead them safely out of all extremes. This Old Landmark is a deceptious guide. To those who have not been deceived, and carried away by it, we recommend the True Guide, the word of God, carefully studied and sedulously followed with earnest prayer, in the spirit of peace, humility, and love.

The trial of Graves tested church polity at the point of congregational government of the church's own affairs and in the limitation of denominational authority in the affairs of a church. The trial revealed the rigid authoritarian spirit of Landmark's founder. With perceptive insight Howell saw clearly and reported responsibly that any disparagement of the pastor's leadership was an affront to the church and to the community.

13

Polity and the President

The official Convention career of R. B. C. Howell is unique in the history of Southern Baptists. Three other men (P. H. Mell, James P. Boyce, and Jonathan Haralson) presided over more sessions, but Howell was elected to the presidency or the vice-presidency almost every time Southern Baptists met during his lifetime (1845-1867). The only exceptions were when he did not attend—in 1863 in wartime when the Convention met the second time in Augusta, and in 1867 when his final illness from a stroke prevented his attendance at Memphis.

Twice in his absence from the meetings, at Augusta in 1845 and at Charleston in 1849, Howell was elected a vice-president of the Convention. He also served as president of the Bible Board with offices in Nashville, of the Foreign Mission Board, and of the first Sunday School Board of Greenville, South Carolina. At the old soldier's last Convention session, in Russellville, Kentucky, in 1866 Howell led the closing prayer. Thus, for its first twenty years, 1845-1866, Howell was consistently on the Convention's official roster, as president, vice-president, or president of one of its boards. No other person in Southern Baptist life has made such a record of continuous Convention service.

In those years, Convention officers were elected by ballot without any nominating speeches. When the Convention assembled, the immediate order of business was to elect the officers to serve only in the sessions of that year. Recurringly Howell was elected to preside on the first ballot, except only in 1857 in Louisville, when he was reelected on the second ballot.

Almost certainly by this date, the Landmark influence was the factor which caused the hesitation of the delegates to reelect until the second ballot. And certainly, as has already been recorded earlier and will claim attention once more later, it was the pestering Landmark problem which provoked Howell's resignation after his fifth reelection in Richmond in 1859. But even after his resignation at Richmond, again in 1861 Howell was elected a vice-president in the very next biennial meeting in Savannah. Evidently Howell was a man of such manifest leadership that his peers unerringly looked to him when they needed a competent man in the presiding chair.

A most ticklish parliamentary chore for the presiding officer during Howell's tenure as president was the I. J. Roberts case at Montgomery in 1855. A carry-over missionary in China from the old Triennial Convention, Roberts from the beginning was a trial to the new Foreign Mission Board. His personality quirks, chiefly at the point of getting along peaceably with his fellow workers in the Orient, cost the Board many trying administrative hours in correspondence and conversation. Finally, the firm disciplinary decision of the Board in relieving Roberts was reported in 1855 at the Convention in Montgomery and spread over seventeen pages of fine print in the Convention annual. It was a boon to the Mission Board's cause that no lesser man than Howell was in the chair at the time.

Reelected—and Then Excused

While this case was ticklish, the Landmark influence was near-tragic. Almost certainly that influence was present in the election of the president in Louisville in 1857. Before two years had passed and time neared for the next biennial meeting in Richmond, Landmarkism was *the* issue. Landmark brethren plainly declared that they had had enough of being shunted away from responsible positions in the Convention structure. They were determined not to be ignored in Richmond in 1859.

Graves had charged that Howell's declared war against Landmark brethren had as its purpose that they (the Landmark brethren) "are to be proscribed from the Boards that direct the great interests

of Southern Baptists." The "war" in Graves' mind was the one
Howell had "declared" in his letter to *The Index* opposing the
proposed Sunday School Union; and the "proscription" was
Howell's objection to the men Graves had nominated to the board
of managers of the proposed Union.

Now as the Richmond convention neared, Howell had reason
to fear that the publication of *Both Sides* and of Graves' editorials
in *The Tennessee Baptist* were designed to block the seating of
delegates at Richmond from Howell's Nashville church. Graves
had succeeded in doing this at the Concord Association and at
the annual Tennessee and North Alabama Convention. Howell's
rugged six-foot frame trembled at the then likely prospect of such
a Landmark success.

J. M. Pendleton, outspoken with the other two of the Landmark triumvirate, A. C. Dayton and Graves, "anticipated a stormy
session at Richmond," especially over the seating of Graves and
Dayton. The report of the Bible Board, now under attack from
many quarters, would surely provoke lively discussion. Pendleton
promised to give his readers in June, following the May meeting,
"a review of all the falsehoods." He said that he himself was prepared to speak "two days and three nights" in Richmond and that
at least one hundred others were ready to hold forth as long if
necessary.

Caught in this bind of threats and fears, Howell anticipated the
upcoming Convention election in personal agitation, day and night.
He would not allow the Nashville quarrel to become the frame of a
Convention squabble. At the same time, he knew that Landmarkism had widespread effect which the Convention could not
ignore. Finally, he resolved his awful dilemma in a bold and
singular way. When his wanted reelection came as a vindication
to his well-known position and as a clear halt to Landmark's
militant march, Howell did a thing which has never been known,
before or since, in Convention life. He resigned.

Graying red hair bristling and long whiskers trembling, he
stood before the 580 delegates and firmly stated his carefully prepared resignation. Almost certainly every delegate entitled to a

seat in that historic assemblage was in his place at that eventful
moment. It was an attendance more than twice as great as the previous high in Convention history. Not until twenty-five years later
(1883), when the Convention met in Waco, did the registration ex-
ceed that record of 580 in Richmond in 1859.

Certainly Howell was pleased at his reelection. A man of justi-
fiable pride, he had been honored and gratified to be called to the
chair repeatedly, although there seems to be no evidence that he
had ever campaigned for the office. Now he knew that his lifelong
struggle to set forward the Baptist cause in the Southwest was directly related to his reelection, but at the same time he was just
as certain that that grand overall lifetime purpose could not be
served by his continuance in office. He had the perception to see
these realities, and he had the stature to act accordingly—albeit
painfully.

Who Won the Battle?

What effect did his admirable action have on the issues at hand?
Certainly neither Howell's resignation as Convention president, nor
his church's expulsion of J. R. Graves from its membership could
stop Graves. The man—that is, Graves—had a contentious spirit (the
bull-headed certainty characteristic of Landmarkism, as it was of
Campbellism, and still is of other like authoritarian literalism). That
spirit could not be exorcised by any one hard encounter.

So when one asks, "Who won the battle, Howell or Graves?" the
honest reply has to be, "Neither." Howell continued in strong
leadership, both in his church and in the Convention. Graves, too,
to the end of his day, in his flamboyant and assertive style, held the
ear and the eye of Southern Baptists. He made his acknowledged
way in their halls and on the Convention platform. Witness his
famed hours-long address to a packed house in Waco, and even after
a near-fatal stroke his "chair talks" throughout Tennessee. The
influence of a man who knew what he believed and was fearless to
speak it for untiring hours to spellbound audiences cannot be gain-
said.

But one blessed development is apparent after 1859: Never

again, seemingly, did Graves march up and down the land to pick
flaws in the orthodoxy of fellow Baptists. The picayunish authoritarianism which marked Landmark's spokesman before the Nashville church brought him to trial in 1858 and the Richmond Convention vetoed his bid to overthrow the presidency in 1859,
seemed to fade away thereafter. Whether it was the church trial,
or the Convention election, or the destruction of the War, or even
the death of his wife in 1868, one cannot say. It is only obvious
that he mellowed in the latter half of his life, to the relief of a denomination that had been widely irked by his strong-willed polemics
of doctrine and ecclesiology.

One strange indication of that mellowing is his son-in-law's
biography, O. L. Hailey's *Life, Times and Teachings of J. R.
Graves.* In that sketch, not one time does the son-in-law refer to
the Howell-Graves controversy. It is as if Hailey never heard of
the conflict. Certainly, one as close as he would have known of
such a devastating encounter. Could it be that Graves himself impressed Hailey to omit such references in deference to the altered
vehemence of the man in his latter years?

Howell, too, takes on a milder tone after his personal cataclysm
with Graves. Admittedly, it did not appear immediately. Howell
was still firmly set in his position of local church autonomy with
the Mississippi committee in 1860. The Graves episode surely had
some effect to lighten the soldier's fire, and the War added a
further restraining influence to take the steam out of Howell's
energy.

War's Dreadful Effect

What the War did in its sad toll of the church, of its pastor, and
thereby of the Convention cannot be fully calculated. Against
these influences, Howell did express his characteristic independence.
Thrown in prison by Andrew Johnson, the military governor, he
would neither admit any instance of disloyalty as would be implied
in voicing the prescribed oath of allegiance nor bow abjectly in a
plea for release to the one he called a tyrant.

His experience in a Federal prison prompted Howell to ponder the comparison of the Federal government and churches. He wrote in his Memorial that they are alike, especially in the voluntary union of the states and of churches in associations. This is a deliberate relationship for their mutual advantage.

To compel the union, Howell concluded, is to destroy it. No coercion powers, he said, can be applied in either relationship. Each church is separate and independent. Their union with one another is fully voluntary and grants to the association specified rights only. The bond of union is the confidence and love of the churches toward each other.

As a prisoner, Howell was deeply impressed with the potential damage from the use of coercion power to compel a continuance of union. "When a church is dissatisfied," he wrote, "it has the right to withdraw. When it does withdraw, it exercises an admitted right."

Still bothered by the contemplation of coercion, Howell wrote of martial law as an example of compulsion in contrast to civil law. Principles (as written in civil law) he said "are of little worth unless they are carried into practice. If those who have the power to violate them, choose to do so"—and here his barb was intended for Andrew Johnson, the military governor—"rules are like 'cobwebs in the path of elephants.' "

Such a trend toward exercising power because one can safely do so, Howell said, appears "especially in times of confusion and agitation." In such times, he pointed out, "tyrants seldom fail to avail themselves to oppress and enslave the people. Our Constitution knows no martial law. In this country is no such thing as martial law. Martial law is the abrogation of all civil law. Tyranny has no longer any impediment to its full dominion when civil law is superceded by martial law. The people have abdicated all rule. The government has no laws capable of execution. We have no rights. We are a herd of abject slaves."

Howell's strong language was, of course, directed toward what he regarded as political tyranny. Possessed of such feelings, it really is a wonder that a fellow Mason, a Knight Templar in his church, was able to persuade his pastor to write a request to Governor

Johnson for his release. That Southern spirit, Morton Howell wrote
in his Memoirs, prompted Morton's former Yankee school teacher
to say in Boston at the beginning of the War that "my father ought
to be hung as a rebel."

But R. B. C. Howell's comparison of the Federal Government was
with the voluntary association of churches. His insistence was that
such union should be without coercion, fully voluntary.

Gifted in Mind and Heart

The force of Howell's personality to achieve voluntary union is
suggested in an editorial in *The Christian Index* upon Howell's death
in April 1868:

> In intellect, Dr. Howell belonged to the class in whom the
> logical faculties, as distinguished from the imaginative, largely
> hold the ascendancy, but who are preserved from cold ab-
> straction by that strength of affection which renders every
> belief a practical energy—and who, therefore, warm while they
> enlighten, and "kindle where they guide."
>
> Brain-power he possessed in marked degree; but he was
> gifted, in even greater measure, with that more excellent en-
> dowment—heart-power. Genial, urbane, sympathetic, un-
> selfish, perhaps there is no man among us, whose death would
> recall to a larger number, the memory of personal kindnesses
> received at his hands. There may be those who deem that he
> held erroneous opinions on some points; but even they must
> confess that he held none which were not the honest dictate
> of his judgment—none which were unsteady and wavering—
> none which were kept back from frank and fearless utterance—
> none which were not tolerant of dissent and open to correction—
> none which lay out of harmony with the doctrines embodied
> in Evangelical Christianity, or with the spirit it inbreathes.

Morton Howell wrote that his father had a powerful physical
frame, was six feet tall, weighed two hundred pounds, and had
very large hands and feet, sandy or reddish hair and grey eyes.

Another who knew him well wrote that Howell had "the appear-

ance of self-esteem, of self-appreciation, coupled with seemingly
ostentatious manners"—a "swelled and pompous vanity which
made him forbidding and unapproachable." But those who knew
him recognized a "cordially warm and generous nature, nothing
envious or unamenable."

As further examples of his strong self-pride, Howell evidently
had a penchant for self-portraits. Item: still extant are *four* very
fine oil paintings. One great portrait appropriately lighted, domi-
nates the modern dining room of a great-great-grandaughter. Another, even more prized, is an exquisite painting on porcelain.

The Marks He Made

A concise summary of Howell's contributions to the development of the Southern Baptist Convention would include these significant emphases:

The superlative of local church independence and autonomy.
The absolute correlary of limited denominational controls.
Full commitment in time and in energy to the ministry.
Full support by churches of a fulltime ministry.
Specialized training for ministry, both theological and pastoral.
Development of a central seminary by the Convention to provide
this specialized training.

The ministry as partnership of pastor and congregation. Any
disparagement of that ministry is a church offence.

The presidency of the Southern Baptist Convention is secondary
to larger kingdom concerns, not to be sought as a political goal nor
to be hugged as a personal treasure.

Full and free communication with the people through popular
media.

Principles of Polity

The genius of Howell's life found expression in its consistent
definition of the denomination. This he began to perceive in his
early years as missionary in the Tidewater, then as pastor in Norfolk,
followed by denominational leadership in the rapidly developing

Southwest, and filled to the full in the strategic beginning years of
Convention service.

Denominational organization, he saw clearly, had limited power.
Baptist associations, he insisted repeatedly, were not ecclesiastical
courts with authority over the churches. In fact their proper func-
tion was violated when they began to dictate to churches. This
principle of limited denominational authority Howell stated from
the first and reiterated often in *The Baptist.*

In like manner state conventions were without authority over
the associations or the churches. And the Southern Baptist Convention, when it came into being, was never regarded by Howell, even
though he became its second president (or by his peers in leadership for that matter), as having authority over the state conventions,
the associations, or the churches.

The first correlary of limited denominational power is that of
church autonomy. If the denomination has no authority over the
church, then the church must have full power within its own sphere.
As Howell said, the word of the church is final. No ecclesiastical
body rules over it. The church itself acts with full responsibility
in all matters of church government.

Howell contributed significantly also to the second correlary of
limited ecclesiastical power, namely that all religious issues must be
settled at the proper level of responsibility. This Howell illustrated
most dramatically in the Landmark matter when the issue was in-
jected on the floor of the Convention in election of the president.
Howell might even assent in essence to Landmark beliefs and practices, but he would not grant the floor of the Convention as the
proper place to settle the differences. The only proper place to
resolve that matter was in the local church. Howell had become
so deeply involved in Nashville in the Landmark problem that he
saw his reelection as Convention president in effect as plunging the
Convention into the vortex of the Landmark upheaval. He would
not allow it, even though it cost him the Convention presidency.

Howell's resignation as Convention president, after he had been
duly elected at Richmond in 1859, was indeed one of his greatest
services from the standpoint of Convention polity. For emphasis

on a very important point it is well to repeat his key thought
(which is given in full in the Appendix):

> Local troubles . . . have given to my name identity with
> certain great principles in Church Polity. . . . I have
> seen . . . a disposition to convert this Convention into an
> Ecclesiastical Court for the discussion of these principles
> by making them test questions, and thus forcing the Con-
> vention out of its legitimate sphere, perverting its character,
> and jeopardizing the interests to subserve which was the
> object of its organization. . . .
>
> These interests must not be embarrassed by bringing into
> your body questions which do not belong in it, and which
> here you have no right to consider, much less to decide.
>
> The principles which characterize us as a denomination
> are dear to my heart. I love the doctrines of our churches;
> I love the polity of our churches: their independent sov-
> reignity under Christ; they are the doctrine, and polity,
> taught in the word of God. Were this the place to put
> these great principles on trial I would unhesitatingly enter
> the lists in their defence, cost what it might. . . . If on these
> subjects internal conflicts are yet to come, the battles must
> be fought on other fields.

With never a turning back, Howell resigned the presidency of the
Convention and returned after the Richmond sessions to his home
in Nashville. That very fall his church implemented the principle
he had stated so clearly in Richmond. The proper place "to put
these great principles on trial," he had said was not in the Convention. The "troubles" were local, and "the arena for such a discussion" was therefore local. "The other fields" on which such "battles must be fought" were the churches. Here in his own church
which Howell led as pastor the spokesman of Landmarkism must
be brought to task. And that Howell led his church to do soon
after his return from Richmond. He said the historic trial which
ensued that fall was a test of church polity: "This case," he said,
"will

test the polity of the churches. It will either destroy or establish it." According to that polity, a church determines autonomously its own beliefs and practices. It does not look to the denomination to decree them by edict. Moreover, the church also is the final judge in matters of fellowship.

There is a third important correlary to the principle of limited denominational power: to truly serve one must keep under his own personal wishes. In human affairs one seldom witnesses the resignation of the chief position. With our native drives, the more normal ambition is to strive for position. Jesus had some strong words about this common human trait (Matt. 20:26, 27; 23:6; Luke 14:7-11). To Howell, there was something more important in serving the Convention even than being president. He relinquished the prominent position to do something more important. It was a worthy illustration of a good principle of polity where he was, in time and in place. He knew who he was in that compelling situation. He addressed his time and place with consistent dedication. The effects of that ministry are felt still in many significant ways.

When Howell expired the community knew that a great man had fallen. The fatal blow was another stroke following the one that had first felled him in January, 1867. The end came on a Sunday, at the time for morning worship, April 5, 1868.

Newspapers report that a throng that overflowed the church gathered for the service on April 7. It was conducted by Howell's successor, Thomas E. Skinner, on the text Hebrews 4:9. Howell's own final sermon to the church, preached the previous year, had been on the text, "Finally, brethren, farewell. Be perfect. . . . " (2 Corinthians 13:11). the procession to the grave—on a hilltop in Mt. Olivet Cemetery overlooking the winding Cumberland—one editor said "was one of the longest we have ever witnessed in our city."

> J. B. Jeter, pastor in Richmond, wrote in the Virginia *Religious Herald:* He was imperfectly qualified to preside. From lack of knowledge of rules of order, ineptitude in ap-

plying them, or wont of reliance on his own judgment, or from all these causes combined, he was one of the most inefficient presiding officers that we have ever known.

Yet so kind was his manner and so manifest his aim to treat the members of the body impartially, that but little complaint of his administration was heard. It was a striking proof of his moral influence, and of the high estimation in which he was held by his brethren, that he was continued from session to session, in an office for which all knew that he was very imperfectly qualified.

That candid appraisal is given here in appropriate conclusion of this account of R. B. C. Howell's career in relation to Southern Baptists. He was thoroughly human, but he came to the kingdom in beginning times. He knew where he was, in time and in place. He knew who he was in that compelling situation. He addressed his time and place with consistent dedication. The effects of that ministry are felt still in many significant ways.

Appendix

Address delivered at the Southern Baptist Convention, Richmond,
Virginia, May 1859, resigning the presidency of the Convention:

Brethren,

From my heart I thank you for this renewed testimony of your
continued kindness and confidence. Five times in succession you
have been pleased to honor me with this high position. Gratefully
have I received it, and have performed the duties you have confided
to me, very imperfectly I know, but to the best of my ability. Whatever errors I may have committed and, doubtless in an administration
of so many years, some have occured, they were in the head, and
not of the heart. On this whole subject I cherish today, "a conscience void of offence towards God and towards men."

At the close of our session in Louisville, two years ago, I determined that I would at this meeting, decline a reelection to the presidency of this Convention. The influences that led me to this
decision were various. It will be sufficient if I say that, as I thought,
I had long enough occupied this chair, and that to retire and give
place to others would be congenial alike to my feelings, and to my
conceptions of the principles which characterize our churches. The
position is also a difficult one, and has given me constant, and
great anxiety. I was desirous, therefore, to be relieved of a painful
responsibility. And especially as I well knew that there are in this
body, not a few brethren who are much more capable than I am,
of performing effectively its duties.

I was prevented however by several considerations from announcing this determination, as I had intended. Among these I refer to the fact that, since no nominations are made to this office, and since my circumstances without any agency of mine, have become somewhat peculiar, I might, as supposed, seem to decline a position which probably you had no disposition to confer, and thereby render myself liable to the charge of presumption. Prudence seemed to me to dictate the propriety of silence.

And further local troubles, as you all well know, have given to my name identity with certain great principles in Church Polity, which for eighteen hundred years have been dear to all Baptists. I have seen, or think I have, a disposition to convert this Convention into an Ecclesiastical Court for the discussion of these principles by making them test questions, and thus forcing the Convention out of its legitimate sphere, perverting its character, and jeopardizing the interests to subserve which was the object of its organization. I fear that retaining the honor you have now conferred, may be made the occasion of introducing these new and disturbing demands into this body. We have assembled from the whole south, for far other purposes than the decision of questions which belong alone to our churches in their individual, and sovereign capacity.

And still further, this Convention is strictly a missionary association, having as such, in charge interests infinitely momentous. Relying upon your promises of support (under God), beloved brethren and sisters have gone far hence to the gentiles. Some of them are in China, others are in Africa. Some have gone to the Indians, and in how many destitute places are they laboring at home? These interests must not be embarrassed by bringing into your body questions which do not belong in it, and which here you have no right to consider, much less to decide.

The principles which characterize us as a denomination, are dear to my heart. I love the doctrines of our churches; I love the polity of our churches: their independent sovereignty under Christ; they are the doctrine, and polity, taught in the word of God. Were this the place to put these great principles on trial I would unhesitatingly enter the lists in their defence, cost what it might. I would either maintain them, or perish in their overthrow. But this is not the arena for such a discussion. If on these subjects internal conflicts are yet to come, the battles must be fought on other fields. This Convention must confine itself within the boundaries of its constitution, and to the legitimate objects of its organization: the dissemination of the written and preached word of God among all people.

We are called together to ascertain what God has been pleased to do by us, during the two last years, and to consult as to what providence indicates as proper to be done during the two years to come. No feeling of ambition, or of selfishness, influences my heart. Indeed, what may become of me is of very little consequence; but the great principles of the gospel must be preserved; the gospel must be preached to every creature; souls must with God's blessing be saved; the nations must be subdued to the dominion of Messiah; the kingdoms of this world must become the kingdoms of our Lord, and of his Christ. Glorious indeed, is the work before us; fearful truly, are our responsibilities; but what can we do if our counsels are divided; if we are turned aside from the true objects before us? What can we accomplish without the blessing of God? How can we hope for his blessing without union, and harmony, and singleness of heart among ourselves!

Again I thank you for your kindness, and for these reasons beg permission, respectfully and affectionately, but firmly to resign the presidency which you have now again so kindly bestowed.

Pages 179-183 and the bottom of page 186 contain Howell's handwritten speech of resignation as president of the Southern Baptist Convention

Brethren.

From my heart I thank you for this renewed testimonial of your continued kindness, and confidence. Five times in succession you have been pleased to honor me with this high position. Gratefully have I received it, and have performed the duties you have confided to me, very imperfectly I know, but to the best of my ability. Whatever errors I may have committed, and doubtless in an administration of ten years, some have occurred, they were of the head, and not of the heart. On this whole subject I cherish to day, "a conscience void of offence towards God, and towards men."

At the close of our session at Louisville, two years ago, I determined that I would at this meeting, decline a reelection to the presidency of this Convention. The influences that led me to this decision were various. It will be sufficient if I say that, as I thought, I would

179

long enough occupied this chair, and that to retire, and give place to others would be congenial alike to my feelings, and to my conceptions of the principles which characterise our churches. The position is also, a difficult one, and has given me constraint, and great anxiety. I was desirous therefore to be relieved of a painful responsibility. And I well knew that there are in this body, not a few brethren who are much more capable than I am, of performing effectively my duties.

I was prevented, however, by several considerations, from announcing this determination, as I had intended. Among these I refer to the fact that, since no nominations are made to this office, and since my circumstances without any agency of mine, have become somewhat peculiar, I might, as I presumed, seem to decline a position, which probably you had no disposition to confer, and thereby render myself liable to the charge of presumption. Prudence seemed to me to dictate the propriety of silence.

180

~~I take occasion~~ ... ... ~~...~~
~~... ... to assign the ...~~
~~... ... ... again so ... ...~~

Local troubles, as you all well know, have
given to my name identity with certain great
principles in Church Polity, which for e-ighteen
hundred years have been dear to all Baptists.
I have seen, or think I have, a disposition to
convert this Convention into an Ecclesiastical
court for the discussion of these ~~...~~ principles, by making them test questions, and thus
forcing it out of its legitimate sphere, ~~and~~
~~thus~~ inverting its character, and jeopardizing
the interests to subserve which was the object of
its organization. I fear that retaining the ~~...~~
as I have now considered, may be made the
occasion of introducing these new, and disturbing elements into this body, as we have assembled from
the whole South for far other purposes than
the decision of questions which belong alone to
our churches in their individual, and sovereign capacity.

This Convention is strictly a missionary,

association, having as such, in charge interests infinitely momentous. Relying upon your promises of support, (under God), beloved brethren and sisters have gone forth far hence to the gentiles. Some of them are in China, ... others are in Africa ...... Some have gone to the Indians ...... and in how many destitute places are they laboring at home? ...... will ...... printed, not be embarrassed by bringing into your body questions which do not belong to it, and which here you have no ...... to consider, much less to decide.

The principles which characterise us as a denomination, are dear to my heart. I ...... the doctrines of our churches; I ...... the ...... of our churches, their independent sovereignty under Christ; they are the doctrines and polity, taught in the word of God. Were this the place to put these great principles on ...... I would unhesitatingly enter the ...... their defence, cost what it might. I would ...... maintain them, or ...... in this own ...... But this is not the arena for such a discussion

If on these subjects internal conflicts are yet to come, the battles must be fought on other fields. This Convention must confine itself within the boundaries of its constitution, and to the legitimate objects of its organisation; the dissemination of the written, and preached word of God among all people.

We are called together to ascertain what God has been pleased to do by us, during the two last years, and to consult as to what providence indicates as proper to be done during the two years to come. No feeling of ambition, or of selfishness, influences my heart. Indeed, what may become of me is of very little consequence; but the great principles of the gospel must be preserved; the gospel must be preached to every creature; souls must with God's blessing be saved; the nations must be subdued to the dominion of Messiah; "the kingdoms of this world must become the kingdoms of our Lord, and of his Christ." Glorious indeed, is the work before us; fearful truly, are our responsibilities, but

183

Readings in Preparation of This Book

Baptist papers for the years, 1835-1868:
  Baptist Standard, Nashville, Tennessee;
  Biblical Recorder, Raleigh, North Carolina;
  The Alabama Baptist, Marion, Alabama;
  The Baptist, Nashville, Tennessee;
  The Christian Index, Penfield, Georgia;
  The Tennessee Baptist, Nashville, Tennessee;
  Religious Herald, Richmond, Virginia.
Beard, Charles A. and Mary R., *The Rise of American Civilization*
  New York: Macmillian, 1941.
Blau, Joseph Leon, *Social Theories of Jacksonian Democracy.* New
  York: Hafner, 1947.
Brownlow, William Gannaway, *The Great Iron Wheel Examined*
  Published by author, 1856.
Cathcart, William, editor, *Baptist Encyclopaedia.* Philadelphia:
  Louis E. Everts, 1881.
Crabb, Alfred Leland (introduction by), *Seven Early Churches of
  Nashville.*
de Tocqueville, Alexis, *Democracy in America.* New York: Alfred
  A. Knoff, 1963.
Dodd, William E., *The Cotton Kingdom.* New Haven: Yale University Press, 1919.
Drury, Clifford Merrill, *No Ordinary Man, William Anderson Scott.*
  Glendale: Arthur H. Clark Co., 1967.
Encyclopedia of Southern Baptists. Nashville: Broadman, 1958.
Eighmy, John Lee, *Churches in Cultural Captivity.* Knoxville. University of Tennessee Press, 1972.

Fish, Carl Russell, *The Rise of the Common Man.* New York: Macmillian, 1927.

Furnas, J. C., *The Americans.* New York: G. P. Putnam's Sons,
1969.

Fuller, Richard and Wayland, Francis, *Domestic Slavery as a Scriptural Institution,* New York: Lewis Colby, 1845.

Graves, J. R., *Both Sides.* Nashville: Spring Street Baptist Church,
1859.

——*Old Landmarkism: What Is It?* Texarkana: Baptist Sunday
School Committee, 1880.

——*The Great Iron Wheel.* Nashville: Southwestern Publishing
Co., 1855.

Hailey, O. L., *Life, Times and Teachings of J. R. Graves,* 1929.

Horne, Linwood Tyler, *A Study of the Life and Work of R. B. C.
Howell.* Unpublished Th. D. Thesis, Southern Baptist Theological Seminary, 1958.

Howell, R. B. C., *A Memorial to the First Baptist Church of Nashville. Unpublished.*

——*Evils of Infant Baptism.* Charleston: Southern Baptist Publication Society, 1857.

——*Notes on Sermons,* manuscripts, letters. Unpublished bound
volumes. Tennessee State Library.

——*Pastor's Book.* Microfilm of original records. Dargan-Carver
Library, Baptist Sunday School Board.

——*The Way of Salvation.* Richmond: Southern Baptist Publication Society, 1859.

——*The Family.* Unpublished manuscript. Tennessee State Library.
Howell, Morton B., *Memoirs.* Microfilm. Dargan-Carver Library,
Baptist Sunday School Board.

Hutchinson, Paul, *Men Who Made the Churches.* Nashville: Cokes-
bury, 1930.

Langdon, William Caucny, *Everyday Things in America, 1776-1876.*
New York: Charles Scribner's Sons, 1941.

May, Lynn E., Jr., *The First Baptist Church of Nashville.* Nashville:
First Baptist Church, 1970.

Morehouse, Henry L., editor, *Baptist Home Missions in America,
1832-1882.* New York: American Baptist Home Mission
Society, 1883.

Patterson, Thomas Armour, *The Theology of J. R. Graves and Its Influence on Southern Baptist Life.* Unpublished Th.D. Thesis. Southwestern Baptist Theological Seminary. 1944.

Robertson, A. T., *Life and Letters of John A. Broadus.* Philadelphia: American Baptist Publication Society, 1901.

Schlesinger, Arthur M., *The Rise of the City, 1878-1898.* New York: Macmillian, 1933.

Shurden, Walter B., *Not a Silent People.* Nashville: Broadman, 1972.

Southern Baptist Convention annuals, 1846-1866.

Spain, Rufus B., *Three Articles on R. B. C. Howell,* Tennessee Historical Society Quarterly. June, September, December, 1955. *The Trial of J. R. Graves.* Nashville: First Baptist Church, 1858.

Triennial Convention, Proceedings of the Baptist Convention for Missionary Purposes held in Philadelphia in May 1814.

Woodson, Hortense, *Giant in the Land.* Nashville: Broadman, 1950.

Wooldridge, J., editor, *History of Nashville.* Nashville: Methodist Publishing House, 1890.

what can we do if our counsels are divided; if we are turned aside from the true objects before us? What can we accomplish without the blessing of God? How can we hope for his blessing without union, and harmony, and singleness of heart among ourselves?

Again I thank you for your kindness, and beg you to accept my resignation by permission, respectfully, and affectionately, but firmly to resign the presidency which you have now again so kindly bestowed

Date Due

Code 4386-04, CLS-4, Broadman Supplies, Nashville, Tenn.,
Printed in U.S.A.